D0171420

A Kiss

UNDER THE
MISTLETOE

A Kiss
Under the
Mistletoe

TRUE LOVE STORIES
INSPIRED BY THE MAGIC OF
THE CHRISTMAS SEASON

NEW YORK TIMES **BESTSELLING AUTHOR**
JENNIFER BASYE SANDER

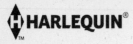

A KISS UNDER THE MISTLETOE
ISBN-13: 978-0-373-89279-2
© 2013 by Jennifer Basye Sander

All rights reserved. The reproduction, transmission or utilization of this work in whole or in part in any form by any electronic, mechanical or other means, now known or hereafter invented, including xerography, photocopying and recording, or in any information storage or retrieval system, is forbidden without the written permission of the publisher. For permission please contact Harlequin Enterprises Limited, 225 Duncan Mill Road, Don Mills, Ontario, Canada, M3B 3K9.

CIP data available upon request.

® and TM are trademarks owned and used by the trademark owner and/or its licensee. Trademarks indicated with ® are registered in the United States Patent and Trademark Office, the Canadian Trade Marks Office and/or other countries.

www.Harlequin.com
Printed in U.S.A.

CONTENTS

CONTENTS

CONTENTS

CONTENTS

CONTENTS

INTRODUCTION

JENNIFER BASYE SANDER

A kiss under the mistletoe? Who doesn't want that? We all long for it, a quick kiss and a tight hug in a hallway, or a longer, lingering kiss in a darkened living room . . . Hmm, it must be December, and Christmas must be coming.

Yes, Christmas is a wonderful time of year, a time when the whole world seems to be decorated with pretty lights and people smile for no reason and do kind things for strangers and exchange really great gifts. But Christmas may also be a time of great strain for married couples—fights over how much was spent at the mall, whose turn it is to mix the eggnog and "What happened to the directions for assembling this bicycle?" It may also be a time of great strain for couples who are dating—lots of time to worry about what type of gift might be appropriate for someone you've only known a few months, questions about whether she should invite him home to meet her parents and whose apartment should have a tree. Oh dear.

Instead, why not focus on the amazing opportunities for accepting love at this time of year? I have gathered up twenty-six stories of love, romance and connections at Christmas from writers around the country. Some are funny, some are sweet and some are heartbreaking, but all of them show that if our hearts are open to giving and receiving love during this special season, incredible things can happen. From a snowy impromptu game of Frisbee in the center of a holiday light display to a woman's trepidation as she arrives home on Christmas Eve with crates of rescued shelter dogs, these stories will help get you in the mood for love in your own life. Blind dates, well-chosen gifts and even a crumpled holiday card can make our hearts sing at a time when our world is festively lit and celebration surrounds us. Look around you—love is there, yours for the asking...

May all your dreams come true and all your romantic wishes be granted.

Merry Christmas!

Two to Tango

TERI WILSON

A breathless four months into our dating relationship and before we were married, my future husband and I gave each other the same Valentine's Day card. I opened mine first, and when I saw the familiar Shakespeare verse on the front of the card, my heart raced.

"What is it?" he asked, narrowing his gaze at the giddy smile on my face.

I didn't bother answering. I just pushed his red envelope toward him. "Open yours."

He broke the seal and his hands froze. He looked back up at me. "We gave each other the same card."

"I know. Crazy, right?" I smiled.

We both smiled.

I don't remember exactly what we said or did next. The details are a bit fuzzy after nearly two decades. But I don't think either of us ascribed any huge, earth-shattering meaning to it. We were in love… so in love that we'd chosen the same special card. We were giddy with the effervescent newness of each other, and now we had a glaringly obvious example of what a perfect fit we were. End of story.

Until it happened again.

The following Valentine's Day, my husband opened his card first. This time, he stared at it for a long, quiet moment before he looked up.

When his gaze met mine, he was clearly shell-shocked. "You're not going to believe this."

"No," I said, reaching for my card.

No way. We lived in the seventh-largest city in the United States. We hadn't even bought our cards at the same store. What were the odds of this happening two years in a row?

Yet when I opened the pink envelope, there I found a card identical to the one I'd chosen for him. Again. Something special was happening. I could feel it. I gazed down at Bouguereau's romantic painting of Cupid and Psyche on the front of the card, and found it more beautiful than I ever had before. I felt as though, like Psyche, I had butterfly wings, and could float straight up into the clouds.

Less than three weeks later, my husband proposed. After I'd said yes and wiped happy tears from my eyes, he told me that he'd known we belonged together the moment he opened that second card. He thought God was trying to tell him something, so he wasted no time before slipping a glittering diamond on my finger.

For years afterward, I held my breath every time I opened a card from my husband. Fifteen Valentine's Days, fifteen Christmases and fifteen wedding anniversaries came and went, but we never again gave each other duplicate cards.

I tried not to think too much about it. Obviously, it couldn't keep happening year after year. That would be impossible. And at least we were still giving each other cards. I knew plenty of married couples our age who'd ceased giving each other cards and gifts altogether. We still did these things.

Granted, after fifteen-plus years it becomes rather difficult to surprise someone. Typically, I chose gifts for my husband that I knew he wanted—things he'd mentioned in passing, or pointed out in catalogs. Until the Christmas I decided to really go out on a limb.

"I'm thinking of getting my husband something kind of crazy for Christmas," I said to my friend, Bess, as we stood in line at the movie theater one chilly December evening.

She glanced up from her popcorn. "Oh, really? What?"

"Tango lessons." I bounced on my toes and waited for her reaction. I was sure she'd be awed.

She wasn't.

There was an awkward pause. Then finally, "Tango lessons?"

"Yes. It will be romantic, don't you think?" I nodded, willing her to agree with me.

"Sure." She snickered into her popcorn.

She didn't sound so sure. In fact, she didn't sound sure at all. And my own certainty began to slip away.

I mentioned the tango lessons to two more of my friends, each of whom had the same reaction. By the third uncomfortable pause, I'd really started to doubt myself.

"Do you think he'll be surprised?" I said into the phone.

My oldest friend, Christy, was on the other end. She'd known my husband even longer than she'd known me, so I figured this was my last chance for someone to tell me what a brilliant idea I'd had. "Oh, I think he'll definitely be surprised."

"In a good way?"

"*My* husband would be mortified. But I don't know . . . yours might actually like it. Has he ever mentioned wanting to learn how to tango?"

I swallowed. "Sort of."

Once.

He'd mentioned it once.

We'd been watching *Dancing with the Stars*, because that's what people who've been married for fifteen years do on Monday nights. It was tango night, which was always one of our favorites. My husband sat on the sofa with a bowl of peanuts in his lap, while I curled up in my chair with one of our dogs.

"That looks really fun." I sighed dreamily at the television, where Derek Hough and his partner were getting their scores from the judges. Perfect tens across the board.

My husband cracked open a peanut and popped it in his mouth. "I read an article once that said ballroom dance lessons will make you fall in love with your spouse all over again."

I slid my gaze toward him, wondering where this thought had come from. Was he just making conversation? Or did he think we needed to fall in love all over again? And, if so, was this the sort of thing we just casually discussed now over peanuts and reality television?

Two years had passed since this short conversation, but I still didn't share it with Christy. "He mentioned something about it once. A long time ago."

"Then he'll probably be into it." She didn't sound altogether convincing.

With only four days left until Christmas, I drove to the ballroom dance school I'd found on the internet. I had to stop myself from taking a detour to Best Buy along the way to buy something safer. What man wouldn't be happy with something like a big screen television? But we already had a giant television. We didn't, however, know how to tango.

The door to the ballroom dance studio opened to a huge, mirrored room with smooth, wood floors. Music filled the air—a cha-cha, if my *Dancing with the Stars* education had taught me anything. There was a tall Christmas tree in the window beside a matching his-and-hers set of rhinestone-bedecked ballroom dance costumes. I tried to imagine my husband in the room, wearing even a few sequins. I failed.

"May I help you?" The man sitting at the desk at the back of the enormous room smiled at me.

I thought about fleeing. Then a couple appeared in the center of the room and started to dance. I wondered if they were married, or if they were engaged and were learning how to dance for their upcoming wedding. Oddly enough, I couldn't tell. When was the last time someone mistook my husband and me for an engaged couple? Had anyone *ever* made that mistake?

As I watched the dancers, a certain wistfulness came over me. I was reminded of my husband's comment.

Ballroom dance lessons will make you fall in love with your spouse all over again.

Seeing the elegant, happy couple glide across the smooth, wood floor, I became a believer.

I wrote a check for a package of four private lessons. It was a sizable check. Not big-screen TV sizable, but close. And the lessons had to be used by March, so if my husband wasn't thrilled with his gift, it looked as if I would be learning how to tango all by myself.

I wrapped the gift certificate in a box, to make it look like any other gift. It sat innocently under the tree until Christmas Eve, and I was sure my husband thought it was something completely ordinary, like a tie or a pair of socks. If my hands shook when I handed him the box, he didn't seem to notice.

He peeled away the wrapping paper, lifted the lid and found the plain white envelope beneath the layers of tissue paper.

My heart hammered as he lifted the seal. He slid the gift certificate from the envelope and stared at it without uttering a word.

"Dance lessons," I said to fill the excruciating quiet. "I thought we could learn to tango. Doesn't that sound fun?"

"It does." He cleared his throat.

My heart sank. He hadn't reacted with horror, as some of my friends had predicted, but he didn't seem exactly thrilled, either. He was pensive. Quiet. Too quiet.

"Here, open yours." He handed me a perfectly wrapped box tied with a silver ribbon.

Disappointment coursed through me as I untied the bow. I'd wanted this Christmas to be special. Different. Romantic.

I opened my gift. Inside was a plain white envelope. As I lifted it out of the box, my heart fluttered in a familiar way I hadn't experienced in a long, long time. I searched my husband's gaze.

"Open it," he whispered.

I did. "Dance lessons? You gave me dance lessons, too?"

He took me in his arms. "I guess it really does take two to tango."

In the soft glow of the lights from the Christmas tree, I kissed my husband. As our lips met, I imagined the two of us dancing on that smooth, wood floor to the dangerous, sultry beat of a tango. And I sent up a silent prayer of thanks that even after all the years, God was still trying to tell us something.

THE DRESS

SHERYL J. BIZE BOUTTE

By the mid-1960s my parents had four school-aged daughters to support and a fifth change-of-life daughter on the way. Birthday and Christmas gifts were often new clothes to supplement outgrown or worn-out school clothes, although we would also get the begged-for doll, bike or skates. Sometimes we got something special: something homemade, handed down or handed over that always gave a unique and precious feel to the celebration.

It was in this tradition on Christmas Day in 1966, while the lights on the aluminum tree changed from blue to green to red and back again, that my mother gave me the gift. Referring to me by my "old soul" nickname, she said, "This is especially for you, Grandma," as she handed me a gold-ribboned box.

Inside was a simple frock; a multicolored, multiflowered shirt-waist dress with a wide belt and a full skirt. It was clearly a gently worn hand-me-down from one of my mother's wealthy acquaintances, but I rushed up to my room immediately to try it on. The bottom of the hem hit just below my knobby knees and fit my still-growing fifteen-year-old body perfectly. It was a spring dress, of course, but I could not wait to wear it to school when the holidays were over.

That next Monday I dressed with a new sense of pride and, in my mind, womanly elegance. My fingers were already turning the front doorknob when my mother's voice called out, "Girl, don't you know it's *January?* You are going to catch pneumonia in that thin little dress!" But I was halfway down the street and around the corner on my way to school before she could finish her warning. My inaugural wearing of this dress would also be the day a seventeen-year-old boy would look out his window from the third house on the right and see me for the first time.

I wore The Dress much too often, but I had never had anything like it. It had the power to make my teenage self feel like a big, grown-up lady, and it quickly became the favorite in my sparse wardrobe. It also made that neighbor boy wait for me to pass his house each day and then fall into step behind me. He walked behind me, stealthily and silently, for the five blocks to school for the rest of the school year. A bookworm and a loner, I was totally inside my own head as I made my way, and I never once thought to look back.

Months later the forces emanating from The Dress would give that boy the courage to ring my doorbell.

"Hi, I'm Anthony from down the street. Does the girl with the flowery dress live here?" he asked the sister who answered the door. Rolling her eyes, she said, "You must be looking for Sheryl. She is always wearing that old-timey dress."

From that day forward, Anthony, the boy who had been my silent and unseen companion, became my boyfriend and, soon after that, my fiancé.

On a beautiful spring day in 1971, we married in the living room of my family home with only our parents, my grandmother and a few friends in attendance. I did not wear The Dress, choosing instead an elegant nonflowery peach chiffon and silk, the perfect complement to my new husband's ruffled peach shirt and coordinating bow tie. Our reception consisted of postwedding photos taken in my parent's parklike backyard, while our few guests dined on crustless tuna and chicken salad sandwiches cut into little squares accompanied by Mumm's extra-dry champagne.

The years passed as we settled into married life, our college graduations, career building and then child rearing. Anthony and I were so destined to be together that people came to refer to us as "Sheryl and Anthony" or "Anthony and Sheryl," as though they could not bring themselves to separate our names. Friends would say, "If you see one you see the other" and actually seemed proud to know a couple that had been high school sweethearts. Our love for each other remained strong and true, but after a time, The Dress that had brought us together became so faded that the flowers were barely visible, and so threadbare that it was no longer wearable. Tearfully, I threw it away.

A thoughtful gift-giver, Anthony would often come home on my birthday, our anniversary or Christmas with a ribbon-tied box containing an exquisite dress, suit or shoes from a small boutique he claimed as his territory for his gifts to me. Once he presented me with a beautiful white suit, and when I asked what the occasion was, he replied, "Because it's Tuesday." He always chose the correct size and only stopped the practice when his boutique of choice went out of business. But of all the wonderful clothes he bought for me, he never found anything as special as The Dress had been.

Then one rainy December day, while flipping through a Christmas catalog, I saw it. A multiflowered shirtwaist dress with a white background, a full skirt and a wide belt. Could it be? I ordered it immediately. When it arrived I was a bit disappointed to find that the fabric had an unworn stiffness, the flowers were not as vibrant and the belt was a skinnier version of its beloved predecessor. But after so many years of The Dress drought, I decided this dress and I would make a pact to stay together, even though we both knew the relationship would never be ideal.

Anthony loved me in this dress, even though I knew it for the poseur it was. And because he loved it, I wore it to work and out to dinner. I wore it to the movies and to the supermarket. I wore it with a shawl in the spring and with boots and a jacket in the winter. I continued to wear it after our daughter was born in 1977, and I was surprised yet happy that, after I punched an extra hole in the belt for just a bit more room, it continued to fit. I wore it through my daughter's early school years and into her entry to junior high. After she told me how much she liked it, I wore it even more. Still, through all that, this dress could not convince me that it was The One.

Since I could never get enough of how happy it made my family, over time the dress and I had settled into an easy truce. I came to accept the fact that it could not help me to recapture the feelings I had had when I wore the anointed original. And it seemed to know that, although it was not The Dress, my family's reactions would make it a most treasured piece.

After nineteen years of wear, I put the dress on one day and discovered I could no longer easily button it. Could I loosen the belt, perhaps? No, I had run out of room for more belt holes. Not wanting to give in to the truth, I buttoned the dress and fastened the belt anyway, breaking a fingernail to the quick as I did so. The dress countered my determination with sharp and intense rib pain that took away my ability to breathe. We stood at loggerheads in the mirror for a few seconds before I gave in and feverishly began to free myself from its grip. My disappearing waistline and the dress had finally conspired to betray me. With mixed emotions, I knew we would have to part ways.

As loved ones became new angels and babies were born, so too my Christmases came and went. They were always special and filled with the joy of being with family and friends. Christmas Day would always find my famous Creole gumbo bubbling on the stove and my homemade cinnamon rolls in the oven.

Christmas Day 2010 Anthony presented me with a large golden box wrapped with a golden bow. Weeks earlier we'd decided that because we felt so blessed, we would forgo gift buying that year. I was both surprised and somewhat annoyed that he had broken the pact and, with pursed lips, I launched into a protest, "But I thought we weren't going to . . ." Smiling that same smile he'd worn on my parents' front porch so many years ago, Anthony waved off my objections and said, "Just open it!" I peeled off wrapping paper printed with the words "Zell's Vintage" and opened the box.

Inside was a simple frock.

A multicolored, multiflowered shirtwaist dress with a wide belt and a full skirt.

With moist eyes and a choke in his voice, Anthony whispered, "No matter how many years pass, you will always be the girl I followed to school." Anthony and Sheryl and Sheryl and Anthony were still here, and The Dress was once again back for Christmas.

TWO TREES

CHELS KNORR

My husband, Tyler, and I have two different ideas about the nostalgia of Christmas trees. He remembers Douglas fir. I remember polyvinyl chloride. His were carefully chosen. Mine was 90 percent off at Target's after-Christmas sale. He remembers the aroma of pine. I remember the smell of dust from the attic. This means that my first real Christmas tree–shopping experience was in the Home Depot Garden Center when I was twenty-five and a newlywed, and still trying to figure out how I, we, wanted to do this "Christmas thing" as a new family.

I have listened to my husband tell many stories about Christmas as he tries to show me why having a real Christmas tree is so important. He tells me about being bundled up in the bed of the pickup truck with his sister. He tells me about visiting five or six lots to find the perfect tree. He tells me about complimentary candy canes, and his father, spinning the trees around like ballerinas for his mother to examine. He tells me about returning to the first lot trying to find the almost-perfect tree they had passed on a few hours before, when their standards were higher.

From my understanding, shopping for a real Christmas tree is a lot like shopping for IKEA furniture—buying it is only half the process.

Tyler and I carry our first Christmas tree inside and put it into the cleanest room in our house, despite the mess of dirt and sap and needles. He tells me about his father holding the tree, and the impatient conversations between his parents trying to get the tree to stand up straight, about his dad crawling to tighten the eyebolt screws against the trunk, only to have the tree move and having to start the whole process all over again. He tells me about carols that turned to cussing after untangling, stringing and restringing the lights. These quibbles don't taint Tyler's memories of Christmas, though. They don't lessen his buoyant nostalgia.

At my house we left the lights wrapped around the tree from year to year just to avoid this process. Having an artificial tree all my life was a remedy for more than just my dad's allergies. It was a remedy for conflict. There was no cold. No indecision. No mess. And with the lights already wrapped, no fighting. Conflict, I believe, would have strained my family's Christmas memories, so we created our own version of nostalgia. The American family stereotype of Tyler's experience is so sharply contrasted to my, also very American, experience. Mine didn't involve getting a new tree every year. There was no process of starting over.

So here I am, the second Christmas as a married woman, and we're Christmas tree shopping at Home Depot in the cold. I'm told this isn't the way tree shopping should be. We're not bundled up, this is our first and only lot, and there are no candy canes. But it feels real to me. The place is covered in pine needles and it smells like Christmas. We haul the tree home and bicker about whether it is standing up straight and which way to face it so the bald spots don't show. We wrap and rewrap the lights. We try to evenly space ornaments and smooth the wrinkles in the felt tree skirt.

I am seeing there is something refreshing about tree shopping every December, year after year. Real trees are forgiving. We start from the beginning, with clean carpet and pungent pine. We do not have to reexamine the mistakes of last year's light wrapping. We do not have to breathe the dust of past errors. Each year we get a blank slate.

We don't have kids yet, so I'm not sure how this Christmas thing will work once we do. I do know we will continue to have a real Christmas tree—a new one each year. We will unfold our own traditions. There will be bundling, and scouting and leveling and decorating. We will argue about whether it's straight and about bald spots. But we'll never argue about the process of starting over.

Velveteen Boyfriend

MARSHA PORTER

At nearly sixteen, I was in love with an older man. Richard, with his long, dark-brown hair and soulful brown eyes, was nearly seventeen. He was the strong, silent type, and I was a talkaholic. I loved to share every detail of my day at my all-girls high school during our nightly phone calls. He said little, offering an occasional "Yeah" or "Sure." For all I knew, he could have been walking away from the phone to watch a ball game and only returning to offer an intermittent affirmation.

It was at my first high school dance, more than a year before, that we met. After that, we were an item and, though he lived on the other side of town, we managed to see each other every week.

My sophomore year, I focused many of our one-sided conversations on the English teacher I adored, Sister Margery. We were reading *The Catcher in the Rye* and the theme was being real. I jumped on Holden's antiphony bandwagon and began ferreting out any phonies in my school or the world at large. Naturally, I shared my observations with my beloved, and even a grunt from his end of the line encouraged me to continue with details and examples galore.

If Holden's descriptions of his boarding-school classmates wasn't an advanced course in phoniness detection, then his New York odyssey made the distinction between fake and real even more clear.

I was convinced that Sister Margery, who seemed to see into the hearts of her teenage students, was a mystical mind reader. The discussions she led made us squirm, question and grow simultaneously. It was the children's novel *The Velveteen Rabbit* by Margery Williams, though, that hit the idea of being real right out of the ballpark for me. I told Richard that my teacher brought a book full of pictures to class. It looked like it was for kids, but I assured him that it contained very adult themes.

I was so impressed by Margery Williams's classic that I couldn't stop talking about it. I even wondered if my inspirational teacher was the same Margery who'd written it. When I found out she could not have been born when it was originally published in 1922, I was sure that her chosen nun name, Margery, was a tribute to my now-favorite author.

I began to quote, paraphrase and adapt Williams's ideas in my nightly talkathons with, or perhaps *to,* Richard. I used these ideas to convey my growing love to him. The very idea that someone on the other end of the line was allowing me to share my every thought, from the inane to the insightful, was irresistible. Today I'd compare it to the crush one develops for a counselor or psychiatrist.

I'd say, "The book says 'When a child loves you for a long, long time, not just to play with, but *really* loves you, then you become real.' That's just like us! We've been together forever (nearly a lifetime: fifteen months), and we do so much more than play (translation: make out). I mean we're on the phone every night and, when we're together, we take long walks, watch movies, hang out with friends and dance. Ergo, our love has to be real!"

Richard would usually offer a one-syllable response that I took as complete agreement. He certainly never argued with me about any of my elaborate comparisons, and I loved that about him.

Next I moved on to the hurt in a relationship. Just as the Skin Horse had explained to the Velveteen Rabbit that becoming real hurts sometimes, we had experienced our share of pain. I didn't appreciate it when his mother insisted that he take the daughter of her friend to a dance, and he didn't like it when the star discus thrower invited me to his junior prom. I was convinced that dealing with pain had strengthened our love, making it more real.

The tear of the Velveteen Rabbit when he was about to be destroyed in the bonfire punctuated my point. Having this true emotion led to the rabbit's freedom and made him real to everyone. Likewise, our relationship became real to everyone when they saw us work through problems and become ever closer.

My *Velveteen Rabbit* obsession was one of many phases I went through that year, and I was not sure that Richard was especially moved by it. I was wrong; apparently, he had been listening rather closely.

On Christmas Eve, he brought me a big white box tied with a shiny gold ribbon. Inside lay a beautifully illustrated copy of *The Velveteen Rabbit* and a stuffed brown bunny with pink satin-lined ears. I hugged Richard, realizing he was actually a very good listener who understood that the book meant so much to me. Our hug led to a kiss, but he surprised me by being the first to pull away.

"You missed something."

Confused, I looked inside the now empty box. "What?"

He pulled one of the floppy bunny ears toward me. I realized that the tip had been squeezed together to hold something. Leaning in to get a closer look, I gasped. There was a delicate gold ring with a heart cut out in the center. Within the heart was a tiny diamond. It was a promise ring—all the rage at the time. Carefully pulling it from its pink satin lining, he placed it on my finger saying, "You were right about us...our love is real."

PERFECT PRESENT

CHARLES KUHN

The significance of my purchase that day didn't register on me at first.

I had spent more time than usual asking questions, trying to understand the explanations thrown back at me. Mutely, I nodded to the descriptions of pixel density, lens size, battery life, brightness and opaqueness as if fascinated by every detail. Truth be told, I wasn't.

Only one thing interested me. The price. "What was the price?" I fumed inside as the saleswoman droned on and on. I know that we men get a bad rap for not being sentimental gift givers, but in this case I really had a good reason.

Could I afford it? That was the question that I needed the answer to. Two weeks left before Christmas, and I had a set budget for this. The money had been squirreled away specifically for a gift for my wife. I knew if I didn't use it soon, the funds would be used for any one of a hundred other expenses waiting in line this time of year.

I had already taken care of the main gifts for the kids, but what about wrapping paper, stocking stuffers, pet toys that would be ripped apart in hours, if not minutes? Who knew how much those would cost? That's why these funds were reserved, emblazoned with bold black letters in my mind, for Melissa's gift. My wife, Melissa. I hadn't asked her what she wanted for Christmas. That was always a risky proposition, but one well worth taking this year.

My wife. It was still hard to believe. This was our first Christmas as a married couple; we'd just been married earlier that year. No big deal, except I was in my early fifties and she . . . well, suffice it to say that she was younger than me by a few years. We had both gotten out of failed long-term relationships and had met online through a political activism website which, considering that we lived in differ-ent states, made our long-term relationship even more special to both of us. It scared me sometimes, to stop and think about the odds, the long shot of our ever connecting. What would my life be without her?

The idea for her gift had come to me through long conversations with her about her likes and dislikes, previous hobbies, childhood experiences, secret ambitions and the usual silly, but memorable conversations spent in getting to know each other. Long ago she had enjoyed photography and, after a lot of encouragement and persistent badgering, had shared some of her best photos with me. She was clearly talented. I was confident in her abilities and wanted her to again pursue something that obviously meant so much to her.

Persisting in my queries, I'd learned that she had given up pho-tography because in her last relationship she had come into constant criticism. She was told the shot was from the wrong angle. Or the light wasn't right. That the picture would turn out horribly. Tired of being criticized, she simply gave up. She finally sold her camera and, it seemed to me, she lost part of herself.

I listened as she told me the story. I heard the pain, the lost moments and the desire to take pictures again. I knew right then that I could change that part of her life and help restore her creative spark.

The next day, I went online to research digital cameras. It was new, it was exciting and it quickly became my Christmas mission. I watched holiday flyers, keeping a stringent eye out for sales and descriptions of cameras that met my requirements. On a Wednesday, I spotted the perfect camera for her. The next two days, I dropped casual comments about our need to go Christmas shopping that weekend.

We made it to the mall on Sunday. We separated inside, each heading off in our own direction, she on foot, me in my wheelchair.

This was another special ingredient of our relationship. After our first few e-mails I had explained to Melissa that I had multiple sclerosis, although I worried that this would spell the end of what seemed like the glimmerings of a love relationship. It never stopped her or scared her away. At our first date, I walked into the restaurant for lunch using a cane and promptly knocked over a strategically placed ornamental tree. We laughed, shrugged our shoulders and enjoyed the remainder of our first date, full of stories and laughter.

Now, three years later, my MS had progressed. My cane was traded in for a wheelchair, and our amusement and comfort had turned to enduring love.

Of course, by the time I wheeled myself up to the camera counter that Sunday afternoon, the camera I had targeted was already sold out. That brought me to the endless discussion I found myself in with the long-winded clerk. In the end, my budget could still handle the new selection, and I left that day feeling proud of my purchase and certain my bride would be happy.

Christmas morning rolled around, and I had managed to keep my secret. My wife unwrapped her gift and fell silent. She cautiously opened the box and extracted her new camera, never saying a word. Attaching the strap, she placed it around her neck. After fidgeting with the camera for a few moments, Melissa leaned in to me, placed her arms around my shoulders and pulled me to her face until our foreheads touched. She whispered, "Thank you. You have no idea what this means. You've just given me back a piece of myself I thought I'd lost forever."

In the days ahead, Melissa pursued her revitalized passion with zest. She photographed migrating snow geese in northern California, soaring hawks in the Central Valley, incredible blooming flowers in our neighborhood, scenic old-growth oak trees in the local park, towering pines in snowstorms in the Sierras and so many more loves in her life. Her photo gallery grew on a daily basis, as did her belief in herself. There was a mutual growth of our bond together, knowing we could help each other heal and rediscover faith and trust. It was a gift of renewal to last a lifetime.

CHAINS OF LOVE

JENNIFER BERN BASYE

Oh, I can see your face now, Dear Reader. Blushing a bit and thinking to yourself, "Oh no, is this one of *those* stories? The kind I keep
hearing everyone else whisper about…?" Rest easy, my dears. There
are no mysterious billionaires with helicopters and handcuffs in this
tale, and I am far from a young college coed just learning about the
world. No, far from it…

   As a girl, my happiest moments were those when I'd snuggle
under the covers in my small room at the top of the stairs ("It's the
maid's room, you know," I would tell my friends on the school play-
ground, hoping to conjure up a sad *Little Princess* sort of life in their
minds), listening to the sound of the rain on the roof. My father would
play the piano at night and the sound would drift up to the second
floor. He'd play Beethoven, Bach and sometimes a little Brubeck if
he was feeling jazzy after a long day at the office. And then, done
playing, I could hear him turn the heavy lock on the front door on his
way to join my mother for the night. Mmm, I would sigh to myself,

that is what my life will be like when I am grown. I will have a big house and a grand piano and children asleep upstairs, and they will know how much I love them and protect them when they hear the sound of a door lock turning for the night.

Well . . . does life ever turn out the way we think it will? In some ways my life does look an awful lot like my parents' life: I live in the same town; my friends are the children of their friends; Beethoven, Bach and Brubeck still comprise my personal sound track. But in many ways my life is far different. My parents smile and laugh and enjoy each other's company; theirs is a model marriage in all respects. And while my own marriage resulted in two delightful boys and a sixty-year-old ski cabin in Tahoe, it did not last a full two decades. Which brings us up to the present, and my sudden need to be over the mountain and through the trees a few days before Christmas.

"Okay," I told my sister, Anne, on the phone, "I can still come to the Father-Daughter Christmas lunch at Dad's club, but I will have to leave right after they clear the plates. The heater is out in Tahoe, and I have renters coming for the next two weeks. The Christmas and New Year's renters offset the mortgage payments in a big way, so if I don't get an electrician in there, I'm in trouble." Anne and I have been going to the holiday lunch with our father since we were little girls in velvet dresses and patent-leather shoes. She'd come down from the Pacific Northwest especially to be there this year, so at least I wouldn't be leaving our eighty-five-year-old dad sitting alone at the table.

The weather forecast looked . . . well, it looked bad. And it sounded bad when I called the recorded highway conditions line to see what they had to say about what was going on in the Sierras. Winter storm warning. That is never really the moment that you want to head up a narrow road in the forest by yourself, even if you are a woman with a four-wheel-drive Jeep.

"Have you checked the weather yet?" David, my boyfriend, asked me on the phone. "What is it supposed to be?" I was quiet. I knew exactly what the weather held, and I also had a good idea what he would say when I told him. David is a worrier. In the time we'd been a couple, I'd listened to him worry about his three grown sons, about his garden, about his Suduko score, about his roof, about his . . . you get the idea. He worries.

"Oh . . . I think it will snow," I finally offered up, closing the window on my computer that predicted a heavy storm a few hours away. "But, hey, the Jeep is four-wheel drive. So I should be just fine." Maybe I downplayed the severity of the forecast a bit, but I needed to be in South Lake Tahoe, and having him tell me I shouldn't go was literally not something I could afford to hear.

I dressed carefully for the luncheon, choosing a warm, knitted wool dress and tights (a great underlayer if I ended up getting stuck on the summit for the night), a silk scarf (I could use it to wave for help if the Jeep went into a snowbank), low-heeled boots (because no one should drive in the Sierras in stilettos) and a cashmere throw (something to snuggle under if that whole spending-the-night-in-the-car thing came to pass). My timing was tight enough that I planned to jump in the car and head straight from the club parking lot to the freeway. It is usually a quick two-hour drive to Tahoe, but with a storm warning, who knew. I figured I'd have at least four hours of daylight in which to make it safely to my little red house in the woods.

"Call me before you leave," he said, in his low and even voice. How I love the sound of his voice, so calm, even when he's worried. He is a large man, my David. It's not hard to squint and see the young college football player he once was. We met years ago in a bookstore, when I thought the big blond man was just pretending to be interested in books so he could flirt with me. He wasn't flirting with me, and he wasn't pretending to be interested in books. Now, becoming a couple so many years later, it looked as if we might have the rest of our lives to sit side by side and read together.

I fidgeted through the luncheon, delighted to be with my father and sister but distracted by my concerns about the weather. Finally, the music program reached a pause where I thought I could slip out without attracting too much notice. In my family, you don't walk out while someone is playing the piano. "Thanks for the lunch, Dad. See you Anne," I whispered. "Be safe," she whispered back.

"Okay, I'm headed up now," I told David on my cell phone as I snapped my seat belt on and adjusted my scarf. No reason to look frumpy on the road. "I know you're in a hurry, babe," he replied, "but please stop off the freeway near my office. I have something for you. Meet me at the gas station just off the exit. I'll be in my car."

He has something for me? I smiled as I put the Jeep in gear and pulled out of the parking lot toward the freeway entrance. It was still a week before Christmas—what could he be giving me this early? I let my mind wander as I drove, imagining all manner of bejeweled finery. Maybe he wanted me to wear something special to his office party. Maybe he'd seen me turn back to that magazine ad for diamond studs last night. Maybe a new watch to help me stay on time for dinner? Or maybe . . . as I pulled up, I saw him standing next to his car, right where he said he'd be. Hmm, empty hands, not a gift bag in sight. What could this be about, then, I wondered as I pulled in next to him and parked. David made a quick gesture with his hand, telling me to roll down my window. I did.

"Here, I went out at lunch and got you this," he said, reaching into his car and pulling out a black canvas gym bag. Didn't look much like a jewelry bag to me, unless it was one heck of a large strand of pearls. He set it gently on my lap as I sat behind the wheel. "Go on, open it," he urged.

Raising my eyebrows at him, I slowly unzipped the bag to reveal . . . tire chains. Chains. Big chains for a four-wheel-drive Jeep, the kind that will get a girl through any kind of weather system. He smiled sheepishly, then said, "Yes, I know your car is fine, but I just wanted to make sure you were prepared for anything. I hear there's a storm coming in."

"Oh, David. Thank you. Thank you so much," I leaned toward him for a kiss. Here was the man I'd imagined all those years ago, the man who would prowl the house at night to make sure everyone and everything was safe and sound. The heavy lock on my heart clicked shut, with David safely inside.

Short and Sweet

Judy Stevens

The holidays were a twinkle away as I did my best to recover from surgery. My days were filled with range-of-motion exercises, pain medication and naps. I needed something fun, something to think about other than myself. It had been two months since my surgery, and everyone was tired of my being sick and in pain, myself included. The chemo had compromised my immune system, so I spent a lot of time at home. But at that point, I just had to get out. Go somewhere, do something, other than dealing with my newly diagnosed cancer.

In mid-December, Ron, my husband of just two years, my teenage daughter and I took our nine-month-old infant to the church Christmas party to see Santa. We were so excited to put the baby in Santa's lap for that special first time. Walking around the gym–turned–Christmas wonderland, I relished the feel of her solid little body in my arms. She was so adorable in her little maroon-and-pink dress with the butterflies on the hem. Her beautiful blue eyes were as amazed as a nine-month-old could be.

"Do you think Isa will sit on his lap or cry?" I wondered out loud as we stood waiting our turn. She was at that age when babies put everything into their mouths. That age when they reach out to pull on hair. Grabbing at my hair as it swung into her face, she pulled, and out it came. I looked down. Her tiny hand was full of my hair.

I handed her to her father and, feeling sick to my stomach, I stumbled a little on the hard gym floor and found a seat on the bleachers. "This has to stop," I said to myself as I sat there trying to compose myself. "The chemo has kicked in, and my hair is all gonna fall out."

My head hurt. Not just on the inside, but the very roots of each hair screamed whenever anything touched my head, and this tiny baby tug was no exception. My head was also flooded with worry—*Will I be alive to see Isa turn one? And my older kids—they just lost their dad two years ago. They can't lose me, too.* Sitting there in the gym on that hard gray metal chair, my stomach churned.

"Honey, are you all right?" my husband asked as he took a seat beside me. I could only stare at him, barely hearing as the Christmas carols and happy faces swirled around me.

At last it was our turn with Santa, and the minute we were done I knew I needed to go. Driving home with the baby safe in the back seat and my husband at the wheel, I said out loud, "Oh please, God, just one more Christmas. I can't have a bald family photo." My husband just looked at me. "Yep," he said, a note of firmness in his voice. I stared out the window into the gloomy December day. Yep, please.

The month passed day by day, and as Christmas approached I hurt more and more. The chemo was working its way through my system. Bit by bit my hair fell out, leaving odd areas still covered. Christmas cards arrived, many with handwritten personal notes, saying, "I am so sorry to hear...", "We were so upset when your mom told us..." and the "I know what will make you feel better, if you just..." I knew they meant well, but it was all too much. Tossing another card into the woven basket next to the tree, I thought, "Can't anyone just wish us a Merry Christmas with our new baby?"

The next week was a blur. A wintry blur of feeling icky but still trying to enjoy the holiday and making the best of the time we had together as a family. Both teens were off school for two weeks but were saddled with caring for me and the baby. With busy teens we didn't get much family time anyway, and they were resentful, angry at me for getting sick. My daughter complained to everyone while my son stood silently in the wings. I knew this was extra-scary for them; they couldn't lose another parent. Sometimes when you are ill, it just hurts the people you love too much to look at you.

Christmas Eve I did my best to look good. I tried my hair one way, I tried it another, but it was just not cooperating. "I hate this," I muttered to myself. "I have to do something drastic." In frustration I chopped my long hair short as best I could, which, since I could really only use one arm, turned out not to be very good. Choppy and uneven. My daughter's expression of shock and dismay said far more than her simple, "Oh wow, Mom."

My husband came home from work and, although it was clear that he noticed what I'd done, kindly said nothing. Christmas Day arrived and we were up early as usual. The smell of a special holiday breakfast turned my stomach, but everyone else enjoyed it. As the time approached to go to my mom's for dinner and the family photo, I grew increasingly frustrated at how horrible and lifeless I looked. My color gone, my hair a weird choppy cut and the huge black circles under my eyes left me in tears.

"I hate being sick! I hate my hair!" I railed against the turn of events as I tossed party clothes around the bedroom when I should have been getting ready for the family dinner. My husband walked into the bedroom, and I exploded again about how horrible my hair looked. "Well," he said, "why don't I cut it like mine? We could be twins, like those couples who wear the same T-shirts," he joked, trying to get me to laugh off my rage. His head is shaved clean. But his solution only elicited more tears and frustration from me. "Why don't you take a quick nap before we leave," he suggested. "Maybe that will help you feel better."

I lay down gingerly beside the baby, and my head stung as it hit the pillow. When I woke, Isa had her hand in my hair and was kissing my head. She sat up, covered with the short hairs from my head. "This is it," I thought, "the end has come. Merry Christmas to me."

I managed to get through the dinner at my mom's, but when we got home that night, I pulled my husband aside. "Cut it off, cut it off now!" I demanded. My hair, my long beautiful hair, had been such a source of pride my entire life, but I just did not care anymore. It hurt too much and, even cut short, it was falling out everywhere. "You're joking, right?" he asked. "You don't really want me to shave your head?" Tears filled my eyes as I nodded. "Yes. Take it all. Shave it clean."

Ron reached for his electric razor. "Wait," I said. "Isa needs to watch. She might not know who I am if she suddenly sees me without hair." "Good point." We sat her on the floor as if it were just another moment of baby play. He chuckled and joked with me as he shaved, "So, shall we try a Mohawk first? Or I could do fun designs like the athletes do?" His jovial attitude brightened my sour mood, and the baby laughed and giggled at the sight of her parents' silly talk.

I sat in that bathroom watching in the mirror as my new husband shaved every single hair off my head. Gone was the cute skinny paralegal he had married two short years ago. In her place was a cancer patient, sick and weak. Ron didn't seem to notice. "See, we are twins after all," he teased. "People wouldn't be able to tell us apart." I smiled. "Also, think how much we will save now that you won't be buying fancy hair products." I smiled again. "And," he continued, holding my chin in his hand and gazing at me with his blue-gray eyes, "hair or no hair, you are beautiful." Who would have ever thought that the most romantic thing a husband could do for his wife would be to ever-so-gently shave her painful head for Christmas?

Five years have passed since that Christmas. Isa is six years old. I am healthy. Once again I have a full head of hair, but it is lovely to know that Ron would love me even if I didn't.

CHRISTMAS BLIND DATE

SUZANNE LILLY

I'm late. Again. Why can't I ever be on time? My internal guilt chided me as I pressed my foot harder on the gas pedal. It was a sunny Saturday, two weeks before Christmas, but from the Arizona heat wave, it felt more like early summer. Watery mirages shimmered above the blacktop as I sped down the rural road to my sister Diana's house. I wished I was skiing in a parka instead of wearing shorts and a cotton top.

I'd overslept this morning, in part to recover from a Friday night blind date gone doubly wrong. After that holiday nightmare, staying single forever looked like my best choice.

I pulled onto the dirt road, trailing a fishtail of dust behind me. My niece and nephew ran out of the house to greet me when I arrived.

"What did you bring us?" Grange peeked in the back seat of my old Chevy.

"It's a surprise." I gave him a hug. "You'll find out soon enough, in exactly two weeks."

Emma stood back, shaking her head. "He always tries to sneak peeks at the presents under the tree. He's going to get caught and get in trouble someday."

I put my arm around her shoulders and gave her a squeeze. "That will be the year he gets plenty of coal in his stocking, won't it?"

She laughed. "He deserves coal this year."

"I do not!" He pulled the gift-wrapped boxes out of the car. "Look at me now. I'm helping her carry all the presents into the house."

Emma snorted and rolled her eyes, trying to act more mature than her brother. "We have a surprise for you, too." She linked her arm in mine.

"I can't wait to find out what it is."

My sister stepped onto the porch, wearing a flour-covered apron and wiping her hands on a dish towel. "If you weren't late, I'd go into shock. I started the baking without you."

"Hi, Sis. Love you, too." I kissed her on the cheek, catching a whiff of cinnamon and ginger. "I have to stay true to form, you know. Never less than thirty minutes late."

She shook her head, a perfect replica of the head shake Emma had just given Grange. "Come on inside. My cookies are almost ready to come out of the oven."

I stepped inside the front door, and right away noticed the man sitting on the couch. How could I miss him? His tall frame and confident, relaxed posture made him look as if he'd just stepped out of a calendar photo. My brother-in-law was nowhere in sight.

"Where's Chad?" I asked Diana.

"Working. He got called in this morning. Being a volunteer firefighter means he's out saving the world more than he's here." She smiled her mischievous smile, always a cover for one of her schemes. "This is Brandon. He's a friend of Chad's."

Brandon's smile lit up his blue eyes. He held up a hand to greet me. *No ring on his finger. Too bad I'm done with blind dates.*

I nodded in return and gave him a half smile. "Pleasure to meet you." Taking Diana by the elbow, I led her toward the kitchen. "Let's go check on those cookies."

As soon as we rounded the corner, I put my hands on my hips.

She spread her hands wide. "What? I told Brandon he didn't have to wait for Chad, but he insisted on staying."

"Diana, I had the worst blind date in the history of the universe last night, and now I walk into your house, and there's some strange guy sitting on your couch. You could have warned me."

She reached in the drawer and pulled out a rolling pin. "He's not strange. He's actually kind of cute, don't you think?"

"How long have you known him?"

"He got stationed here at the Air Force base a few weeks ago. Chad met him at work, and they found out they have a lot in common. He's very nice."

I washed my hands and grabbed the rolling pin. "Give me that. I'll roll out the cookie dough. It'll release some of my tension."

"What happened last night?" She took a ball of gingerbread dough from the bottom shelf of the refrigerator and handed it to me.

"You will not believe what Heather did to me. She invited me to her house, for a casual holiday dinner."

Diana's hand covered her heart and she gasped. "Spare me. How could she be so cruel and invite you to dinner?"

"Just wait. When I walked in the door, there were not one, but two guys sitting at the table. I got the impression they'd been waiting for me. They both smiled, and one actually patted the chair next to him."

"Let me guess." She tipped her head and put a finger on her chin. "You were late."

"That's not the issue here." I flattened the dough with a hard slap and smacked the rolling pin on it.

"You'd better let me do the rolling before you kill my gingerbread men. Get yourself some eggnog. Add some extra nog, too."

"I'm serious, Diana. One guy had yellow teeth that stunk as if he hadn't brushed in days. I don't think he'd brushed the three hairs on his head, either. The one that patted the chair was painfully prim and proper. He never relaxed or cracked a smile. Those three hours turned into the longest dinner party I've ever endured."

"Did you tell Heather you didn't appreciate her 'surprise'?" Diana raised her fingers in air quotes.

"Not exactly. I didn't want to hurt her feelings. She doesn't believe me when I tell her I'm not interested in a relationship. While we were rinsing the dishes, she asked me which guy I liked better."

Diana set the rolling pin aside and began cutting the dough into shapes. "Sienna, you and Mark split up over a year ago. Don't you think it's about time you dated again?"

It had been exactly thirteen months, eleven days, and oh, let's see, about twenty-one hours since my boyfriend had decided to move out of our apartment and into his new girlfriend's house. It wasn't something I could let go of easily. I'd been badly hurt, and I was scared of opening myself up to emotional pain again.

"Maybe I *will* have that eggnog." I turned around to walk to the refrigerator and almost bumped into Brandon. My skin prickled as I breathed in the same air as he did.

He held out a baby bottle. "Could I have more milk? Little Andrew woke up, and now he's snuggling on the couch watching Spider-Man with me."

Way to melt a girl's heart. "I'll get you a new bottle." I put the empty one in the sink and got a new bottle out of the refrigerator. As I removed the lid to warm the milk, Brandon leaned back against the kitchen counter and crossed one cowboy boot over the other. His T-shirt couldn't hide his rock-solid abs. My cynical side went into high alert, warning me that someone like him was too much to hope for.

He's probably some grifter with an agenda.

"I'll take the bottle to Andrew." I twisted the cap back on, grabbed a plate of frosted cookies and carried both to the living room.

"Ooh! Look at the candy-cane cookies!" Grange left his post as Christmas Tree Gift Inspector and ran to the table. He picked up two cookies, handing one to Brandon. "Here you go, Uncle Brandon."

"Thanks, Buddy. Your mom makes terrific cookies, doesn't she?"

Uncle? Since when did my nephew call men he'd just met Uncle?

My niece opened the drawer of an end table and pulled out a deck of Uno cards. "Want to play?" she asked me.

"I'd love to, Emma. Playing a few card games with milk and cookies sounds terrific. Why don't you put on some jingle bell songs?" I said.

"It doesn't get better than this," Brandon said as he carried the cookies to the dining room table to join us in the game. I wanted to dislike him and I was ready to find any fault, but he was making it difficult to do so. His easy sense of humor made the card game the best time I'd had since long before Mark left me.

I'm an accountant because the concreteness of numbers and lists gives me a sense of order and safety. I like the same thing in my personal life, so I started a mental list of pros and cons for Brandon.

Pros: He likes kids, he's in great shape and he tells funny jokes.

Cons: Hard to think of any. Considering my decision to stay single, that's not a good sign. Make more effort to find some bad habits.

When Diana turned on the Christmas tree lights, and the kids complained that they were hungry, I realized we'd been playing cards and chatting for hours.

"Oh my goodness! It's almost six o'clock. Let me order a pizza," I offered.

The kids settled in on the couch to watch a holiday movie while they waited for the pizza to arrive. Brandon and I set the table.

"Since you're in the Air Force, you could be living anywhere in the world. Why are you here in rural Arizona?" I hoped he'd tell me he'd gotten into trouble so I could get my "Cons" list started.

"I came home early from a tour in Germany because my grandmother is sick. She's living with my mom, and I wanted to be close so I can help out as much as possible."

Double darn. He'd added another item to my "Pros" list. But he didn't stop there. He added two more "Pros" when he told me he loved skiing and cooking. Those things put him over the top.

"How about we get together next weekend and go skiing? This time of year the night skiing is spectacular."

I paused for a few seconds, pretending I might have something better to do. "I'd love to."

"Great. Afterwards, I'll cook dinner for you."

"What type of cooking do you do?"

"My specialty is a secret family recipe for green chili enchiladas." He leaned back in his chair. "Would you like me to make them for you?"

I breathed in deeply to calm the flutter in my heart. I had the same sensation I get when I'm at the top of a mountain, looking down at the ski run, the minute before I push off. It's a mix of excitement, fear and anticipation.

I nodded. "I'm ready."

"What did you say?" His eyebrows drew together.

A flush of heat rose from my chest to my cheeks as I realized I'd spoken my thought out loud. "I'd love to have enchiladas with you." At that moment, I realized I wanted to share enchiladas with this man for the rest of my life.

He smiled, a bright, warm smile that rivaled the lights on the Christmas tree behind him. I started falling down the mountain, slipping off the icy, snowy slope of my singleness.

The night ended far too early, and I left for the long drive home. As I backed out of the drive, Brandon stood in front of my sister's house, waving to me until Grange pulled on his arm and dragged him back into the house.

My phone rang almost as soon as I closed the door to my apartment.

When I picked up, his smooth voice came over the line. "Do you think tomorrow is too soon to have those enchiladas?"

"Unfortunately, it is. I'm going car shopping with my dad tomorrow."

"Oh." He couldn't hide the disappointment in his voice, which made me strangely happy. "Then how about the next night? You can show me your car, and I'll feed you."

As much as I already liked Brandon, this seemed to be moving too fast. I stalled and mentioned something about a busy week. We agreed to the dinner date the weekend before Christmas.

The week after Christmas we went skiing. I met his family in the middle of January. By Valentine's Day, I had fallen so deeply that in my heart I knew he was my perfect match. In March, we sent out wedding invitations for an April wedding.

"I've never seen two people fall so crazy in love at first sight," Diana commented as she helped me put on my wedding veil.

"I never believed it could happen." I turned away from the mirror and hugged her. "Thanks for the holiday blind date, Sis."

Twenty-five years later Brandon and I are still cooking together. His enchiladas are still just as good as the first time he made them for me. I still laugh at his jokes. And I'm still amazed at how our Christmas blind date turned out to be such a perfect gift.

Snowy Christmas in the Park

CHERIE CARLSON

I had never seen so much silverware—six forks, six knives and six spoons per person, polished and gleaming and set in a proper constellation around the plate and on the linen napkin before me.

"How can we use them all during a single meal?" I whispered to my husband, Bill. He smiled back reassuringly. We settled in to our chairs at a round table for eight, nodded greetings to our table companions and vowed to give it our best effort. The wine was poured and the feast began. Leaning toward Bill as he sat next to me, I whispered, "Happy Anniversary."

First up, a smooth and spicy carrot soup with crème fraîche. I ate slowly (certain that I had picked the right soup spoon), savoring both the creamy soup and the sumptuous scene that surrounded us. An elaborately printed menu described all the delights still to come. Shrimp and scallop timbale with horseradish and a cognac sauce. For the main course a Peacock Pie, a Boar's Head and a Baron of Beef. This Christmas feast happens only once a year. And this year was our thirty-seventh wedding anniversary.

I'd read about this event for years; the *Wall Street Journal* called it the "World's Premier Christmas Dinner." Held every December in Yosemite National Park, it began back in 1927. The nature photographer Ansel Adams produced it until 1973, and since then members of the Fulton family have continued the tradition, adding choirs and fine music, drama and frivolity to a feast and theatrical event that lasts close to four hours.

The setting is magnificent—the dining room of the Awahnee Hotel is transformed into a Gothic-type cathedral with stained-glass windows, a Parson and the Squire's table beneath. Actors wear period costumes with vibrant colors of purple, turquoise, rich black and scarlet, gold trim and velvet, fluffy sleeves and flowing fabric. It looks like an Italian painting come to life, the perfect setting for a romantic holiday dinner for any couple. I'd anticipated it for months now, and here we were.

"Comfy?" Bill nodded yes to my question. I reached over and adjusted his shawl-collared sweater, pleased with how handsome my husband looked. Most of the other men in the room were in black tie, but tuxedoes are no longer an option for Bill.

Planning a romantic getaway should be easy; just choose a place, book it and go. But life, particularly travel, is not as easy now as it was in our earlier years. Twelve years ago Bill became disabled. Now he's wheelchair-bound and that leaves it to me to do all the packing and unpacking, driving, checking in, tipping and carrying suitcases—the things most wives expect their husbands to help with. I also load and unload the wheelchair, help him transition from the car to the chair and then push him wherever we need to go. And we decided together that we needed to go to the Bracebridge Dinner for our anniversary. So there we sat amid all this silverware and countless courses to come. I offered up a silent prayer, a request for one perfect night in a romantic setting.

The three-day trip had gotten off to a lovely start. The day before we'd driven through the agricultural part of central California. Under a clear and sunny winter sky, I was delighted by the sight of Angus cows in field after field. I was raised on a cattle ranch and am still fond of the cattle my father liked to call "black roses." Closer to the park entrance, the road was lined with giant trees reaching to the sky, casting their green everywhere.

We'd reserved a little cottage with a spectacular view of the waterfall. Yes, it was everything I'd hoped. After unpacking our finery for the feast, we headed over to the Awahnee to scout out the scene for the big night to follow. Bill and I would both feel more comfortable if we had a chance to survey the scene beforehand and spot any potential pitfalls for the wheelchair.

The hotel's Christmas decor was suitably grand. A huge Christmas tree dominated the lobby, densely decorated with the glossy sheen of large red balls and silver ribbons. All around us were relaxed and happy winter vacationers, taking pictures of themselves in such an impressive setting and enjoying warm drinks by the enormous stone fireplace. Live music added to the gala atmosphere.

"Bill, this is lovely! I'm so glad we gave this a try." He quickly agreed, taking in the scene before him. Surrounded by a relaxed and friendly crowd of strangers in the lobby, we chatted pleasantly with one or two standing nearby. I can understand my husband when he speaks, but not everyone can.

"Yes," I repeated to him as we headed back to our cottage for the night. "This is going to work out just fine. Tomorrow's dinner will be a dream come true."

The drive through the dark back to our cottage gave me a chance to review the route for the following evening. I am always on the lookout for what might go wrong. Sadly, there is so much Bill cannot do, and, yes, sometimes I am overwhelmed with the responsibility I have for both of us. But life is short, and we refuse to stay at home all the time and feel sorry for ourselves. God has given us an amazing world, and I want to do all I can to help both of us enjoy it.

Next morning we woke to an inch of snow on everything. The mountains were spectacular, and the waterfall right across from us sounded like it was dropping icicles. It was cold, white and beautiful. The huge trees now resembled white statues, reaching out to us with their branches like the arms of God.

Snow. What so many dream of for their Christmas can be a big challenge for us. Snow. Ice. Cold. Slippery. Instead of going to breakfast together, I bundled up and went out to pick up coffee and breakfast. Better we stay inside and simply enjoy the dramatic view from our window until night came.

Almost too soon, it was time to get ready for the long-anticipated Big Evening. I always plan at least two hours for preparation, but after those two hours, Bill looked so handsome! After thirty-seven years of marriage and a severe handicap, I still love and appreciate this man. Not every man would be game to go out in his wheelchair on a snowy evening in an unfamiliar place.

Off we went to the hotel and the Bracebridge Dinner in our finery. The trumpet blew a herald to announce the start of the dinner, and the assembled diners entered the hall of magic, music and amazing delicacies. Huge tables with tall candelabras stood before us. We were escorted to our places by the cast of players, dressed immaculately in colorful costumes.

The room grew dark once everyone was seated, and out of the darkness came a commanding voice.

> *Let all mortal flesh keep Silence*
> *And with awe and wonder stand.*
> *Ponder nothing earthly minded . . .*
> *As the Light of Light descendeth*
> *From the Realms of Endless Day . . .**

In the darkness I felt my husband's hand take mine and give me a gentle squeeze. Such a familiar touch after all these years of marriage. The lights came up again and the feast was on. Throughout

---

* Bracebridgedinner.com

the long meal, we hardly saw our plates removed before another one was placed before us with yet another tempting course. For hours on end we were transported into another time. The chorus sang with gusto. The jester made us laugh. The room was dressed like a medieval cathedral with stunning stained-glass windows and boars' heads. What fun to leave behind cares and concerns and real-life handicaps for a few hours and just enjoy life, the Christmas season and the happiness all around us. It was long and dreamy, it was romantic and sweet. And too soon it was over.

We left the warm and welcoming room with reluctance, heading back outside into the night and a cold sky. The drive home was only a mile or so—what could go wrong?

Driving slowly along the route to our cottage, I spotted an animal on the other side of the road. A large tan and furry something was blinded by my lights and standing stock-still. I steered toward him so that Bill could help me decide what it was. Lights flashed behind me. The park police. I rolled down my window.

"Did you see it, too?" I said to the man who approached. "Was that a wolf or a coyote? I can't tell . . . " The officer tilted his head in confusion.

"Ma'am?"

"By the side of the road—didn't you see it? A big animal. I was trying to get a better look at it."

"Oh, we thought you were drinking. Could you get out of the car and do a few simple tests for us, please?"

It seemed that I had been driving on the wrong side of the road. I passed the test and climbed back into my car quite humbled.

"Happy anniversary, dear," I said to Bill for the second time that night, putting the car back into drive and continuing on. It was just a small blemish on that perfect evening I'd prayed for. But the night was almost over, and there had been no disasters.

Parking the car in front of our cottage, I went to get Bill's chair from the back. He opened the door to move onto the chair, and as soon as he set his feet down on the ice, he slid right to the ground. Dress shoes and ice—why hadn't I realized that would be a deadly combination? I can do a lot of things for him, but I can't lift Bill off the ground by myself.

"Hang on, I'll get help," I said, taking a deep breath to calm myself as I walked as fast as I safely could across the ice toward the hotel, hoping that someone would be available this late at night. Soon two security guards came around a corner, and together we got him up and into his chair and into our warm room. Thankfully, he wasn't injured; he had just a bruise and was very cold from sitting on the ice as I went for help.

For thirty-seven years now, we have lived and loved together and have only grown more patient with each other's faults and failings. We both believe it is a privilege to serve each other and that every day is a gift from God. That night, as we kissed and snuggled together, I held Bill, gratefully appreciating his eternal patience, his courage and his endurance. As I closed my eyes that night, resting in the arms of my loving husband, I thought back to the message in the closing song of the dinner:

Now the joyful bells are ringing.
All ye mountains praise the Lord!
Lift your hearts like birds awinging,
All ye mountains praise the Lord!
Now our fes'tal season bringing
Kinsmen all to bide and board.
Sets our cheery voices singing,
*All ye mountains, praise the Lord!***

** Bracebridgedinner.com

FROZEN FRISBEE

RUTH BREMER

Alex and I met in college and started dating in December of my junior year. But instead of calling it dating—not wanting to jinx it, I suppose—we just said we were "hanging out."

We "hung out" quite a lot in those last few weeks before finals and the holiday break, and whenever we got together it always involved some sort of unconventional activity. No dinner and a movie for us. We dressed up in goofy clothes and played a round of golf at the public course—although neither of us had ever golfed before. We walked along the train tracks at night sharing a sixty-four-ounce fountain drink. We cooked dinner on a barbecue grill at the park, using only a pocketknife and a spoon, and ate our baked beans straight from the jagged-edged can. So when we were invited to a Christmas party, we couldn't just show up on time with seven-layer dip like normal people.

It was the first major snowfall of the season, so naturally Alex decided it was a perfect opportunity to fire up the grill and barbecue some burgers. We agreed to meet up later that afternoon and cook a stack of hamburgers to take as our contribution.

The snow fell all day long, and we both got tied up running holiday errands on the snowy roads, so ultimately we had to scrap the burgers-cooked-outdoors idea. "So . . . we could make some punch instead," Alex suggested before leading me up and down the grocery store aisle grabbing 7-Up, cranberry juice and a bunch of fruit. "Do these folks even have a punch bowl?" I asked as we stood in line. He shrugged. "We'll find out soon enough."

Punch ingredients in the bag, we were on our way to arriving at the party on time. But to my surprise Alex soon pulled off to the side of the road and parked. "Are we there yet?" I asked, looking out the window at a snowy park.

Every December, the city put up an elaborate display of lights in the park along a major street near campus. It was impressive: huge letters that spelled out "Happy Holidays," Santa with his reindeer and sleigh, elves, skiers, snowmen, gingerbread houses and giant candy canes. I smiled. "Oh Alex, you remembered!"

A few days earlier I'd mentioned how much I loved that massive spectacle of festive decorations and looked forward to it each year.

He nodded. "I remembered. And I thought we could play a little Frisbee," he said, turning off the car and opening his door. Yes, I was touched by his thoughtfulness, but . . . "Um, it's really cold out there. And I am so not dressed for this."

"No problem! I have noticed that you seem to run on the cold side, so look at this . . ." Reluctantly I got out of the car. Shivering in the dark I peered into his open trunk. "I brought everything I had in the closet—something will fit you." Yes, he had an entire selection of extra coats, hats, scarves and gloves. "So, Frisbee then?" Yes, Frisbee. Why not?

Bundled up against the cold, we ran through the pristine drifts toward the display towering above us, casting its colorful lights onto the shimmering snow. We flung the Frisbee back and forth in front of the elves and candy canes while car after car drove by, on their way to dinner or the shopping mall or their own holiday party.

Soon enough our Frisbee game morphed into a snowball fight. I forgot all about being cold and just gave in to the fun. We laughed and ran around until the snow soaked through our shoes and our fingers grew numb and even Alex didn't want to be cold any longer. Then we packed it up and headed over to our friends' house with the heater blasting. We arrived at the party an hour late, out of breath, our clothes still damp from the snow. Punch bowl? No, but another guest did manage to find a big bowl that we could use to mix our ingredients.

Alex took me home after the party. "Tonight was great, Alex. Frisbee in the snow, amazing." He looked at me closely. "Do you like doing crazy stuff like that?" he asked me. I told him I did. Not fully convinced, or maybe fishing to see if I wanted to go out on a "real" date, he continued: "You know, if you ever want to do something normal, like go to a movie or something, we could."

Really, I didn't. And so our "hanging out" turned into dating, then to engagement and finally marriage. Through it all we carried on with our adventures. Spur-of-the-moment scavenger hunts, an impromptu run through the sprinklers and, one summer evening, we had a romantic picnic in the median of the busiest street in town, until an emergency response team showed up, thinking we had been in an accident.

Perhaps it was inevitable that over the next several years our lives—and our dates—gradually became more conventional. We worked, raised babies, cleaned the house, paid the bills and we got tired. Too tired to play Frisbee in the snow or prepare meals at the park. Too worn out to come up with creative new ideas for the rare date night without the kids. We usually just went out to dinner. Every once in a while, we caught a movie.

Year after year at Christmastime, we decorated the tree, hung the stockings, wrapped presents, played holiday music and tried in vain to get all three kids to smile at once for the Christmas card photo. Life was good, but it was pretty darn conventional.

Sure, we've both changed since college, but some things remain the same. He's still thoughtful; I'm still cold all the time. And one common trait we share has remained the same: we're still drawn to the unconventional. We'd rather do something new than something safe. But normal is exactly what we had become.

Seventeen years after we played Frisbee in the snow among the twinkling Christmas lights, we decided to reject normal once and for all. Our kids were older and we weren't as physically tired, but we were still tired. Tired of the rat race, tired of playing it safe for the benefit of some unknown future while we missed out on the present. So we stopped. "Do you like doing crazy stuff?" he'd asked me seventeen years ago.

We gave away most of our belongings—everything that wouldn't fit in a fourteen-foot U-Haul. Alex resigned from his job, and we moved to a small mountain town in Colorado, a place where we had always wanted to live but had discounted as being too impractical. Immediately it felt like home. It's cold, of course, but with enough extra layers of clothing I think I can handle it. I started my own freelance business, and Alex now has a new job—with regular hours, no travel and no work to take home. We're living life on our own terms again, leaving some space for creativity, fun and whatever offbeat stuff might come to mind.

So now it is Christmastime in our new hometown, and all the surrounding towns are lit up with extravagant holiday light displays. I've been scoping out each one and think I have found the perfect place. I've put the Frisbee in the trunk, along with some extra gloves and hats. I'm just waiting for the right night. This time, maybe we'll even let the kids play with us.

THE CHRISTMAS VISITOR

DAWN ARMSTRONG

Sitting on the final suitcase, shifting my weight in all manner of awkward gyrations, arms and legs flailing, I slipped to the floor with a thud. "Crikey, packing for an international trip is never easy, especially with all these Christmas presents to manage." Three gray cats wound themselves wistfully around my legs and the bags, the subtly skillful weave of their scent hiding a secret message for me to come home soon. They took turns sprawling across the clothes in the now-open bag and swatting my hands as I tried to close it again. Realizing that their efforts to abort this latest mission weren't working, they resorted to one of their more successful ploys, looking up at me in pitiful, sad-eyed unison.

Like the craggy teeth of a crotchety crocodile, the zipper slid into place. The cats had lost their battle. For the past two weeks, Silly, Willy and Billy had slept in, climbed over and loudly voiced their catlike objections to the luggage, intuitively understanding that two big bags meant a longer-than-normal absence. I ran my hands over each of the rescued siblings, kneading and tickling them in reassurance. "Clever kitties, don't worry. Mary Fe will be with you while I'm gone. Now, riddle me this: How am I going to get these bags down the stairs, on the shuttle and through the airport all by myself?"

Muttering to myself, I walked through the house performing a final check before heading for my flight. Glancing at the stove to make sure that it was switched to "off," I drew a line through another item on my list. *Is anything else out of place?* Noticing the poinsettia-painted cookie tin sitting precariously near a cabinet ledge, I moved the gift for my house sitter to the middle of the dining room table and readjusted the name tag. "I hope she finds this before my three rascals do!" The most adventurous of the three cats came running into the kitchen as if on cue. "You'll fit right into this family, Willy. We all love homemade chocolate chip cookies at Christmastime, especially Johnny. Every year we make them with his favorite recipe."

The aroma of hot cookie dough, warm chocolate chips and walnuts wrapped itself around me, a cloak of memories flooding in. I paused, gazing up at a picture of the handsomest of men. I rememorized the smallest detail of each adored feature to the finest degree. Plucking the vintage photo from its rightful place among loved ones on the dining room credenza adjacent to the kitchen, I gazed at the young man in uniform. His dark short-cropped hair; heavily fringed, twinkling hazel eyes; strong, yet kind features; clean-shaven face and saucy grin gave comfort even as I accepted the familiar longing that washed over me. "A couple times a year is not enough. I can't wait to be near you again. When I get to Australia, I'll bake a special batch just for you."

A ringing phone jogged me back into the present moment.

"Grandma, I was going to call you from the airport before I got on the plane...Yes, I'm catching the usual flight from San Francisco to Sydney, and then a Regional Express hopper...I'm doing okay, was just thinking of how much I miss Johnny...You were just thinking of him, too? No, I'm not surprised at all...has he visited lately? I can't wait for your and Auntie's fresh mangos and vanilla ice cream!"

I hung up the phone with eager thoughts of the delicious food and relaxing holiday that awaited me Down Under. Mouth watering, I floated on visions of homemade succulent roast, flaky meat pie, creamy layered trifle, rich caramel tart and crisp ANZAC cookies. I mentally catalogued the long-awaited events that the next two weeks would hold: sleep in, tend garden, copy family recipes, cuddle a koala and, of course, catch up with scores of relatives at the holiday gathering.

My family is spread all over, and the annual get-togethers always include a thorough review of our ancestry. Every household attending brings a copy of the book compiled to document the intrigue surrounding births, deaths and great events leading back to the roots of our tangled family tree. The chronicles begin with journeys across the great ocean from England, continue with the first settling of long-past rough-and-ready relatives on the wild continent of Australia and end with the newest American additions. Every year we look forward to reliving our history, and particularly remembering those loved ones who bravely paved the way before us.

Australia, at last. The long plane trip had already begun to fade in my mind as I showered and snuggled down into my own special space on the veranda-turned-guestroom. New curtains and bed linens, I noticed. "Grandma Gloria and Auntie Mavis must have been busy," I said to the empty room. Early afternoon, and the house was warm. I was grateful for the ceiling fan, and anticipating the nighttime breezes the window-lined room would afford. I could hear the quiet sounds of country life in the neighborhood, happily reminding me of my upcoming visit with Uncle Merv to his cattle and cane farm. The voices of my grandma Gloria and her sister Mavis talking softly in the kitchen drifted in.

The two sisters had lived a lifetime of memories since Gloria, as a war bride at age nineteen, first left Australia for America. Separated for over fifty years with only one phone call a week to sustain them, they remained close. Having survived a spouse or two each, the sisters were overjoyed to live together in Australia once again.

My eyelids grew heavy and sleep was near, but I heard my auntie ask my grandmother, "Do you think Johnny will visit? Dawnie will be over the moon if that happens, but gutted if it doesn't. It will be a shame if he doesn't. I wouldn't want anything to put a damper on her visit."

Grandma Gloria answered quickly. "I'm sure of it. He hasn't disappointed her yet, and he stopped by last evening to check in on me. I bought him a new ornament this year, a dancing Santa. You know how much he loves Christmas." I smiled at what I'd overheard, and drifted off to sleep.

**

Like practiced runners preparing for an event, we three women settled into our starting places the next morning, tea in hand, warming up for a marathon of memories, hopes and dreams, set against a backdrop of communal meals, gardening and housekeeping. As if on cue, a slight, gray cat with weathered fur trotted onto the veranda, curled herself around my legs, gave a squeaky purr and settled down in her own special chair.

The crunch of wheels across a gravel drive heralded the first of many cousins who would be stopping by over the next fortnight.

"We had to use the amphibian to get out here today," my cousin Danette announced as she and her daughters walked up to the porch. "Creek flooded the bridge, but the girls and I wanted to get a visit in before school starts back up."

She looked at me and smiled. "So, has Johnny dropped in yet?"

My spirits dropped, though I tried not to let it show. "Not yet, but Grandma bought a special decoration for him. It's a motion-activated Santa. At night when the house is as quiet and still as can be, right before she goes to bed Grandma hears 'Jingle Bells'..."

My grandmother and her sister exchanged a look. "Dawnie, we could use your help in the garden for a bit this afternoon. You can see the new bananas and pineapples that are coming in and we can pick some vegetables for dinner." It was clear that the sisters were trying to change the subject from who had already been by and who had not.

As the sunlight faded, all company departed, and the day came to a close. We three turned to our usual routine of feeding the animals, locking the doors, tidying up and individually preparing to hunker down together for an evening of television, nostalgia and precious moments. Gloria's urgent tone carried across the quiet evening air as we changed into our pajamas.

"Dawnie, you have a visitor."

Goose bumps coursed over our skin as we quickly converged in the middle of the house. Auntie Mavis and I looked at my Grandma Gloria expectantly. A cool breeze ruffled our nightgowns. Gloria nodded toward the back door, which stood wide open, porch light spilling in to illuminate the area around us.

"It's Johnny, isn't it? Where is he?" Auntie Mavis's face paled.

Gloria looked at me pointedly. "Apparently, your father opened the door to let the cats in, fixed the broken porch light and left us a gift."

Eyes widening, I gasped as I looked down at the table in front of me, and saw the family ancestry album opened to the very page chronicling the birth and untimely death of my father, Gloria's son Johnny. Though we were in the dining room, the sound of "Jingle Bells" drifted out from the sitting room.

Mavis looked at Gloria. "Heidi, the little gray cat, is asleep in my bedroom."

Gloria looked at Mavis. "And the big ginger kitten is lying on the porch chair outside. I can see him from here."

I looked at Mavis and Gloria. "It's Dad!" Running into the vacant sitting room, I barely noticed the wildly dancing Santa twisting and turning on his pedestal. Picking up my grandmother's matching family picture of my long-lost father in his military uniform, I twirled in a circle around the room. Eyes watering, heart exploding with love for him, I stopped and planted a breathless kiss on his still cheek. "Merry Christmas to you, too, Dad; I'm so glad you made it."

The sisters stood in the hallway, beaming joyfully. "We knew he would, Darling. Look above you." I looked up and was not surprised to see I was standing directly below the mistletoe.

FIRST CHRISTMAS KISS

SCOTT "ROBBY" EVANS

By mid-December, fog had hung over the northern California valley like a dripping gray shroud for more than a week. I was missing the clean white snow of Pittsburgh—it just didn't seem like Christmas without snow—and I was terribly homesick. More than once, I woke up crying, missing my dad and the life we had before my parents divorced. Every afternoon when I came home from school, I found Mom asleep on the sofa. I guess she missed the snow, too.

One night I was at the kitchen table doing my homework for high school. Mother was, as usual, asleep on the sofa. The table sat under the kitchen window and the curtains were open. I glanced up and noticed our downstairs neighbor, Heather, smiling in at me from outside in the hallway. Except for her glasses, I thought she looked just like Audrey Hepburn in *Breakfast at Tiffany's*.

I didn't want her to see my mother already asleep on the couch so early in the evening, so I hopped up and opened the window before she could get to our front door. Her little daughter, Emily, was, at four, too short to look inside.

"Hi, Robby. Doing homework?"

"Yeah. A little algebra."

"Oh. I hated algebra," she said. The cool, damp air rushed in through the screen, carrying her perfume with it. "I wonder if you could help me."

"You need me to babysit?" She was a young divorcee, and I'd watched her little girl on a few occasions.

"No, I need your muscles. On my way home from work, Em and I bought a Christmas tree. Can you help me carry it in?"

"I'll grab a jacket and be right down."

"You're an angel." She looked down at Emily and said, "Robby's going to help us put up our tree. Isn't that nice?" Nice for me, too, I thought, as I walked past my mother on my way to get my jacket. This would probably be the only tree I'd help decorate this year, as my own family's Christmas didn't seem to be shaping up that way.

On my way back from my room, I leaned over to check my mom. She was facing the back of the couch and her breathing was heavy, so I knew she'd be out for the rest of the night. I draped a faded afghan over her and, buttoning up my jacket, went out to try to grab a little holiday spirit.

The Christmas tree loosely tied to the roof of Heather's car was actually a shrub about five feet tall, far from the majestic seven-foot silver spruce we'd always had in Pittsburgh. But once I grabbed the trunk, I realized it was a substantial little pine after all. I hoisted the tree up to my shoulder.

"Wow," Emily gushed. "You're strong."

I smiled, realizing that the weight lifting I'd been doing after school was paying off.

Once we got inside Heather's apartment, I learned the real reason she wanted my help.

"I'd really like to have the tree in front of the window, Robby, but it means moving the couch out of the way. Could you help me move it?"

The couch sat under the window, facing the bookshelves and TV on the opposite wall. On a side wall was an easy chair and a little table and lamp and, opposite it, was the wall that led down the hall.

"So...where do you want the couch, then?" I asked. She looked around the small space.

"What if we move the chair over to this wall and put the couch where the chair was?"

It would be snug, but we could make it work.

The sofa was heavy—it was a hide-a-bed. We shoved it into place and slid the coffee table in front of it, after moving the little chair and lamp table to the opposite wall. I was sweating by the time we'd made room for the tree, which still rested against the wall outside the apartment.

Heather disappeared and came back with a metal stand and, after covering the carpet with an old towel, she positioned the stand under the window.

"Okay, Robby. We're ready for the tree."

Emily jumped up and down, squealing.

I opened the front door, grabbed the tree and maneuvered it into the stand with ease. Heather, crawling on all fours underneath the lowest branches, tightened the clamps that held it in place.

"Does it look straight?" she called from below.

I stepped back and stood beside Emily. "What do you think?"

"Pick me up, Robby, so I can see better."

I hoisted Emily into my arms and we looked at it together, wisps of her hair brushing my cheek.

"It looks perfect, Mommy."

Heather crawled out from under the lower boughs and brushed off her black slacks as she stood. She stepped to one corner, and then she walked around us and went to the hallway to check the view from there. She smiled.

"You're right, Em. It *is* perfect!"

The room had grown fragrant with the pine scent and, although a little cramped, it seemed very warm and homey. My buttoned-up jacket added to the warmth.

"Thanks, Robby," Heather said. She stepped over and quickly kissed my cheek.

I felt myself blush and grow even warmer under my wool coat. In my fourteen years, no girl had ever reached out to touch me in such a casual way.

"Well, I guess I should get back to my homework."

Heather reached out her arms and took Emily from me. "Can't you stay a bit? I was hoping you could help us decorate."

"Please, Robby," pleaded Emily. "Puh-leeze." Only little girls can draw a word out like that.

I shrugged. "Sure, I guess." Algebra could wait. My grades were okay in that class anyway.

Heather lowered Emily, who stepped over and hugged my leg.

"Let me grab the boxes out of my closet."

"Okay," I said. Feeling a little sweaty, I asked to use the bathroom. "Mind if I clean up a little?"

"Make yourself at home."

I splashed cold water on my face to cool down and then wondered if there was a way I could smell a tiny bit better. Glancing around the room, I noticed deodorant—Mennen—and a small bottle of English Leather aftershave. I used both liberally.

"Wow, you smell good," Emily said when I walked into the living room.

Heather had put a record on—Andy Williams singing Christmas songs—and she was opening a box on the coffee table. She spun around and smiled, saying, "He sure does."

For the next hour, we decorated the tree as if we three were a happy little family. Heather asked me to put the star on top and string the lights, and she helped Emily hang ornaments.

We sang carols along with the record and shared stories as we worked. I told Emily about sledding down the snow-covered hills of Pennsylvania, and Heather promised we'd all go sledding up in the Sierra-Nevada mountains sometime during the break.

As we worked, sometimes Heather's hand touched mine, and she often smiled up at me with light in her eyes. Her perfume, the scent of the tree, Emily's giggles, the warm, dim little room—it was all so intimate, I could barely breathe at times. It was heady stuff for a high school boy.

When the tree was fully decorated, I plugged in the lights and Emily clapped and squealed. The greens and blues and reds and oranges converged on Heather's face. She looked radiant. At that moment, I felt older than fourteen, and she seemed younger than twenty-two.

Standing back, looking at the bright tree together, Heather put her arm around my waist, while holding Emily against her hip.

"It's the most adorable tree," she said.

"Santa Claus will like it, won't he, Mommy?"

"He'll love it," Heather assured her.

"You get more presents if Santa likes your tree," Emily told me, speaking with great authority.

I nodded. "I think I heard that, too, when I was a kid."

"Oh, Robby," she said, "thank you so much for helping us."

Emily yawned and said, "Mommy, I'm tired."

"Okay, Honey. Why don't you go to the bathroom like a big girl and then change into your pajamas, while I say good night to Robby."

"Can Robby tuck me in?"

"Oh, I don't know, Sweetie. We've probably kept him long enough."

"Please, Robby! Please tuck me in."

I shrugged. "Guess I can stay a little longer."

"You hurry, then," Heather said. She set her down and patted her on the bottom.

Heather turned toward me and put her hand on my arm. "If you've got to get back, it'll be okay." Study algebra, or sit in front of a Christmas tree with a girl who'd kissed me on the cheek? It didn't take me long to decide.

"Naw. I can stay a while."

Heather nodded and turned her attention back to her daughter. "I'll go help Emily get her pajamas on."

"Can I have some water?" I asked.

"Help yourself."

I went to the kitchen and filled a glass with cold water, which tasted great. Sometimes the simplest things are the most satisfying. A white-and-red candy, wrapped in twisted plastic, sat on the counter. I unwrapped it and plopped it into my mouth, as if I owned the place.

Then I noticed a piece of mistletoe on the table. Thin red ribbon was tied in a bow around the stem, and a new package of thumbtacks lay next to it. I stepped over and opened the package. Somehow I felt more at home in Heather's apartment than I'd felt in my own.

I stabbed the tack into the stem of the mistletoe just as Heather appeared.

"She's already asleep. She really wanted you to tuck her in, but I picked up her clothes from the bathroom and put them in the hamper. When I looked in, she was sound asleep."

"That's okay," I said. "I can tuck her in some other time."

Heather glanced at my hands. "So, you found my mistletoe."

"Yeah. I mean, I just figured it was one more decoration. You know."

Heather nodded. "Yes, I know." She grinned. "Where should we put it?"

I shrugged. "The hallway, maybe?"

She glanced up. "How about right here? Can you reach the archway?"

Reaching over her shoulder, I pushed the thumbtack into the plaster of the little archway that separated the hall from the kitchen. The mistletoe and the red bow now hung above us.

"Well?" Heather said. "Should we try it out?"

My heart raced as she rocked up onto her toes. Was this really happening to me? I bent down and closed my eyes. Our lips touched briefly. Hers were soft and warm, and my heart did a little flip inside my chest. I pulled away and opened my eyes. Heather's eyes were open, and she was smiling sweetly at me.

"You're so young, Robby. Just think how many kisses there are in your future. And whoever she is, she will be a very lucky girl to have you."

My heart was breaking. Couldn't that girl be Heather? I wanted to stand under that archway for the rest of my life. But, no, I knew that was only a young boy's dream.

"Guess I should get back," I said weakly.

She nodded. "It's late, and you've got school tomorrow."

I looked at the beautiful lights of the Christmas tree for a few more seconds, then stepped toward the door and grabbed its cold handle. I opened it and stood there, hoping she'd insist I stay longer, but she stepped forward and said, "Good night, Robby."

When the door closed, I turned away. My heart was broken, but as I climbed the stairs to my apartment, I knew there would be other Christmases and other kisses in my future. There have been, but the memory of that first kiss still makes me smile. The soft kiss of a young, single mother struggling to find her place had been the best gift I received that year, giving me a small taste of what my future life would be as a family man with a tree and a daughter of my own.

THE SCENT OF PINE AND CANDLE WAX

ILLIA THOMPSON

It had not been a good year for my small family of three. The trauma of an unexpected divorce had shaken my children and myself. Hamid was just twelve and Malina was younger by two years. The idea of moving somewhere new to start over held great appeal. With this in mind, I went on an autumn weekend visit to a small village near Carmel. Could this be a place for us to heal, I wondered, as I walked down the quaint streets and viewed the small shops.

Always a book lover, of course I needed to check out the library before deciding if this town seemed right. And that was where I saw it—the small sign on the library bulletin board that read "Preschool Director Needed." The interview for the position was to be held the very next day!

The interview was quickly arranged. Yes, all agreed that I fit the requirements well, but there were other, mostly local, applicants under consideration. I left my phone number with the interviewers, but tried not to get my hopes up. As I left town, I made a silent vow to myself: if I were to be chosen, my children and I would make the move. The phone rang two months later. "Can you start January 1st?" I could indeed.

Settling into a new community is always hard, but so much went well right away. The parent co-op offered me instant acquaintances so I was spared the difficulty of seeking out new friends. My talents were put to good use on the job, and I felt revitalized. Now, if only my romantic life would fall into place so smoothly, I thought. Friends in my former large suburb had warned me, "Don't move to a small community. They don't have many single men." My reply: "I only need one."

"I found the man I want you to marry. I found the man I want for a stepfather." This was my now-fifteen-year-old son, Hamid, speaking from the back seat of the station wagon as we returned from our first community Thanksgiving Dinner in the country.

"Hmph," I replied, focusing on the still-unfamiliar road home. But he went on, adding a bit of support to his statement. "Really. He plays the guitar and sings and has an orange truck." I dismissed his request, "Now, when we get home, go play outside before it gets dark."

My daughter, Malina, perked up at the mention of a guitar. "He sounds interesting, Mom. Why don't you give it a try?" It was true, I had started dating again, but I certainly did not need my son acting as matchmaker. He persisted and I finally agreed to ask his candidate, Locksin, to join us for a Sunday lunch. Lunch seemed harmless, as innocent as any time could be for carrying out my son's wishes.

Lunch, as it turned out, was delightful. The four of us seemed like an instant family, comfortably visiting over a midday meal and soon after singing and playing board games together. Locksin and I began to spend more time with each other, and I slowly felt the possibility of a new family in the making. But did he feel the same way I did?

This bachelor from southern California, who didn't even wear socks with his Topsiders and who was now working on land as a contractor after being at home on the sea, intrigued me. He of Viking ancestry. I of Mediterranean heritage. He, well over six feet tall, and I, barely five-feet-two. Both of us in our forties. There was an ease between us when it came to sharing our thoughts. Not long after we met, on the ride home after an outing in the nearby redwoods, I suddenly blurted out what was on my mind: "If you asked me to marry you, I wouldn't necessarily say no." Hmm, maybe that was a thought I shouldn't have shared, especially since he didn't respond at all to my statement. Complete silence reigned for the rest of the long two hours back. Locksin dropped me off at my house without a word and drove off into the night.

***

Two long weeks passed. The phone rang at last, with Locksin on the other end. "We have to talk." Over a quiet dinner in a restaurant, he reached across the table and held my hands while finally sharing his thoughts on the subject. "I love your children. I would love to be married. And I would love for us to have a child together." I took that as a proposal. "Yes," I responded quickly, squeezing his hands to seal the deal. We married six months after my son had arranged our first meeting.

Our first December seemed to arrive quickly after we settled into our new home. Hanukkah was my family tradition and Christmas was his family tradition, so of course we blended both the festivities and the worship. Candlelight in the silver menorah, colored lights on the evergreen tree. Traditional Hebrew prayers and Christmas caroling with neighbors. A wreath on the front door, next to the mezuzah, the small ceramic case that holds the Ten Commandments. Presents wrapped in the traditional Jewish silver and blue and Christmas gifts wrapped in red-and-green paper. And, of course, mistletoe hung from the rafters. That first winter as a new family, the roundness of my form showed clearly that our child would be present at our next December celebration. Our son, Lance, was born into a cradle of love. During the December holidays, wide-eyed, this baby took in all the lights. Every year throughout our marriage our blended celebration took place. Until a December came when Locksin was not there.

He'd come home from work early complaining of a stomachache, something unusual for this strong, healthy-looking man. Sixteen-year-old Lance left me a note, scrawled on the back of an envelope: "Dad's not feeling well. I'm taking him to the doctor's. Don't worry. I'm in charge of the situation. Love, Lance."

It was a quick year once his cancer diagnosis was made. For the last three months, his bedside became a place for stories and sharing with family and friends. Alone together in the evenings, my husband

and I talked deep into the night, speaking our deepest truths. On an early June morning, when no one was around, he took his last breath. I later held his cool hand for the last time, remembering his declaration from years ago. "We hold hands well together."

For me, the following December lost its festive feeling. Locksin was gone. No Christmas tree. Christmas Eve found me driving alone past a small nursery. "Should I stop and buy something festive?" I wondered. Red would liven up my gloomy house, add a bit of brightness. The parking lot was deserted; everyone else had long since made their holiday purchases. I wandered through the quiet aisles, trying to decide on a small something. A lovely evergreen wreath sat alone. Pine? No, I needed to stick with something less symbolic of Christmas this year, I thought, shaking my head and walking past it to the poinsettias. Red ribbons tied around red sparkling pots. Just what my living room needs right now, I decided, picking up the one closest to me and heading for the cash register. I glanced down at the wreath again as I walked past. Maybe . . . but no. I wasn't ready yet.

Standing at the counter, I looked again to where the lone green wreath sat near the entrance. Maybe I did need it after all. Something to acknowledge my husband's love of Christmas. He wasn't there with me this year, but at least the house could smell as if he were.

"There's a wreath back there. Just sitting there," I said to the clerk as he wrapped the poinsettia in plastic to protect my car seat. He nodded and began to ring up my plant. Quietly, I asked, "How much is it? That wreath." Again, he paid no attention. "What's the price?" I finally said in a louder voice. "Here's your plant. Where is your car?" he asked. I pointed to the only one in the parking lot.

On the way out, he bent down smoothly and scooped the wreath up with his free hand, never breaking stride. "Merry Christmas," he said quietly, as we walked together to my car. "You can have it." Startled, I protested. "Oh, but I can buy it. You don't have to give it to me."

"Nope," he said, shaking his head firmly. "It would give me great pleasure to give it to you. It's late in the season, and it needs a good home."

With a poinsettia dressed in red and the pine-scented wreath filling my car with the familiar scent of Locksin's beloved pine trees, my holiday spirit revived at last. "Locksin, are you there?" I asked out loud in the car. "Did you do this, dear? Thank you for the wreath." I hung it by the front door, encircled by his love once again.

SONG OF LOVE

DENA KOUREMETIS

There he is, in his tux up on the stage of our local performing arts center. It's our pop choir's fourth performance of the Christmas season. As I peek from backstage at the group singing "It's the Most Wonderful Time of the Year," I see my salt-and-pepper-haired husband, elegantly moving to the beat of this jazzy rendition, not knowing just how very smitten I am with his crooning and how thrilled I am that he loves being up there as well. Smiling and shifting my weight from one patent-leather pump to the other one, in anticipation of my turn onstage, I remember my childhood dreams of the perfect Christmas. It looked just like this. But for many decades of my adult life, Christmas was far from harmonious.

I came from a very close, fun-loving family. We laughed a lot. We traveled a lot. And from my earliest recollection, my two brothers and I made music together, encouraged by two piano-playing, singing, whistling parents. As we embarked on cross-country trips to visit our Midwestern relatives each summer, my brothers and I had our own little band going in the back seat of our family Mercury. One brother was the (voice-produced) bass player, the other was the drum section and I was the diva singer.

As I got older, singing became an important part of my life. My teenage insecurities kept me from auditioning for school musicals or singing in choral groups, so instead I learned to play guitar and imitate my folk-singing heroes of the 1960s in my own, private way. By the time I got to college and gained more confidence, I was sharing my love of singing with my friends, regaling girls in the dormitory with my doleful version of "Leaving on a Jet Plane." I spent a year in Greece during college, and I wowed my Greek relatives by strumming my guitar and singing Nana Mouskouri songs.

On my own in San Francisco after college, I joined my church's Greek Orthodox choir as an alto, learning to sing the beautifully arranged hymns that dated back to early Christianity. It was wonderful to engage in harmony with a group who shared my love of singing and, for many years, it would become my form of worship, lending me both roots to honor and wings to fly.

And then that part of my life suddenly grew silent. I'd married a man who seemed perfect for me. Our daughter came along very quickly, and we were delighted. In time, however, I found that many of the things I thought would never matter much to me began to haunt me. I loved to dance, but my husband didn't. I loved music of many kinds, played piano, played guitar and sang, none of which he felt capable of learning nor appreciated in me. I loved to write, but couldn't seem to get him to read. I was in love with the idea of flying and traveling; he was a white-knuckled passenger. Other differences in taste and especially temperament became evident as well and, before long, laughter faded for good in our house. No matter how hard I tried, I could not reproduce the kind of joy I had experienced in my childhood home.

Christmastime, which had been one of the most special times of the year for me growing up, became a disappointing guessing game about which gifts might be returned. Gift giving was no longer about sharing in a cacophony of delight, surprise and appreciation. What had always been a wonderful time of the year became one of the most upsetting. And finally, after almost twenty years, it all came to an end.

Soon after settling into this new single phase of my life I received an invitation to a friend's surprise birthday party from another Greek-American family. In case you haven't heard, Greeks know how to throw parties. One of the people hosting the party was my friend's handsome brother George—someone I had seen occasionally throughout my married years at Greek festivals, weddings and picnics. I would dive into the long dance lines next to him because of his smooth dancing style and his knowledge of the dance steps for each type of Greek tune. My husband stood on the sidelines, watching, but never seemed to want to join in the fun.

I knew George, a San Francisco firefighter, merely as my friend's brother—a jovial, well-mannered man everyone seemed to love. Good-looking as he was, he had never married, and no amount of interrogating his sister about why he had remained single seemed to produce much of an answer. Now that we were in a more intimate social situation, however, I was able to observe him in a different way. Once the surprise part of the party was over, I looked on as he and his sisters joked and howled as they recounted childhood stories. They recalled lines from movies they had loved, talked about their parents and reminisced about the different places they had lived. Soon I heard two of the sisters harmonizing as they sang a song. It was magic. It felt as if a piece of home had surfaced in someone else's family, and I was just plain happy to be there.

By the end of the party, George was paying special attention to me, but I tried to shrug it off. The ink on my divorce filing was not yet dry, and I had been told by all my well-meaning friends to go it alone for a while. "Get to know yourself," they advised, "apart from being a wife and mother." Yet I was flattered to be getting a new kind of attention from someone I had always been curious about. George walked me to my car and asked if he could call me soon. Without a hint of hesitation, I said yes.

Once he picked me up to take me to coffee a few days later, George wasted no time in letting me know that he had always had a secret crush on me—that his gentlemanly ways, while proper, had merely masked an interest that went back to before my marriage some twenty years earlier. I was taken aback by his honesty and surprised that he would make himself so vulnerable. But I was also interested. And no advice from friends or family was going to stop me from exploring the possibilities of at least having a closer friendship with this man.

Apart from our Greek-American ethnic background, George and I had much more in common than I could ever have imagined. At the time, we (and our siblings) were both caring for aging, increasingly disabled parents who needed 24/7 care. George's mother suffered from dementia, diabetes and heart problems, while my father was failing fast with prostate cancer, abandoning his lifelong love of food and laughter after having lost Mom seven years earlier. Dad passed on shortly before my divorce became final, while George's mom continued needing care for the unforeseeable future. I understood from early on that I would have to share George with his commitment to care for his mother before he and I could truly be together. But apart from the challenges we faced, I was to find that this special man loved to sing and dance; had a private pilot's license; shared my love of travel, art and literature; and had a sense of humor that kept me in smiles nearly all the time we were together. It was an unbeatable list of made-to-order traits I could not easily resist.

Once the divorce was properly final, George began attending church with me, rejoining the choir after more than fifteen years of being away from it. To look over at the tenor section and see George's face as he blew secret kisses my way between Byzantine lyrics made me fall fast for this amazing man. After a year and a half of being together, we announced our engagement and set a date, knowing George would have to commute back and forth to care for his mom after we moved in together.

The wedding was divine. As the church filled with voices singing the ancient music of the betrothal and the wedding sacrament, George and I circled an altar table three times in what is called the "Dance of Isaiah"—signaling the first journey we would take as a couple. The sweetness of having discovered one another in midlife was special enough, but because George was pushing fifty and had never been married before, his relatives surfaced from all over the country to wish him well.

More than twelve years have gone by since that fateful surprise party where we met. George's mom passed away a year after our wedding and, not long after, we bought our first home together. The first Christmas in our new home George retrieved some carefully wrapped and taped storage boxes. Inside was a beautiful assortment of oversized glass Christmas ornaments, most of which were mini-Santa figures he had collected over his bachelor years. Really? Honestly, a single man who collects Christmas ornaments? How adorable is that? I knew no small Christmas tree would do to display these lovely decorations, and each year I use a different combination of them.

But nothing would prepare me for the first Christmas we would sing onstage together. After having seen me sing in a large, well-organized choral group, George auditioned for it as well and got a place in the tenor section. Each year the group puts on a show of amazing Christmas music, both traditional and pop arrangements. For months we prepared for these musical extravaganzas, and we had to learn and memorize the music at different rates and in entirely different styles. And for months we sing and allow the Christmas feeling to envelop us, far longer than most folks get to enjoy it.

So here I am for the first time, gazing at my tuxedoed, dapper husband in the men's section. But it's always the same little ritual taking place. He catches my glance and, soon, a secret kiss gets blown my way. No matter what comes next in the song of life, I know I am with the right partner at last.

ANOTHER CHRISTMAS AT UNCLE JOE'S

JERRY WHITE

"Jerry," said Marie, "I have a niece you should meet." Marie was a hostess at a nightclub I frequented in Fresno. "You two would make a great couple," she continued.

Well, what could I say? "Sure, I would be delighted to meet your niece."

Marie smiled and said, "Donna. Her name is Donna; I will ask her to come by on Saturday night."

Donna arrived at the club Saturday night with two of her girl-friends in tow—safety in numbers, I guess. As advertised, Donna was indeed a beautiful and charming young lady. I asked her on a date; she accepted. By the end of the first date I had proposed to her. There was no question about it—she was the one for me. It was the long dark hair, the soft voice, the warm smile and the eyes that sparkled with a mischievous glint.

"You can't be serious," she said when I proposed. I was very seri-ous, but I figured it would take at least one more date to convince her. I knew what I wanted right away, but apparently she needed more time to reach the same conclusion. In fact, it would take years.

Donna's sister, Carolyn, was getting married soon after I met Donna. At the wedding I got to meet the entire family—and what a family it was. Dena, Donna's mother, was one of nine children, all of whom still lived in Fresno. Their yearly tradition was to gather at Uncle Joe and Aunt Norma's home for a Christmas Eve celebration, and then attend Christmas Eve mass at midnight. Christmas Eve at Uncle Joe's became a tradition for us, even though we were sometimes only dating on and off. Families with Italian heritage know how to celebrate religious holidays—lots of great food, laughter and hugs.

Four years after we met, Donna was working as a nurse in San Francisco and I was on orders for duty in Vietnam as a captain of infantry. We spent Christmas Eve at Uncle Joe's for the fourth time in a row that year, knowing that soon the tradition would be broken. Next Christmas I would be overseas.

After a few months in Vietnam I was reasonably sure I would not survive the one-year tour. I often thought that dying would be acceptable if only I could see Donna's smile, hear her voice and hold her hand one more time. Just one more time, that was all I asked from the war.

Soldiers who had served several months in Vietnam were entitled to a seven-day Rest and Recreation period outside the country. Married soldiers would travel to Hawaii to meet their loved ones. A few days before Christmas I saw a fellow officer and good friend, Lieutenant Chuck Boyle. He didn't look too happy.

"Why so glum, Chuck?" I asked.

"I was going to meet my wife in Hawaii for Christmas, but now she can't make it." He looked at me with a gleam in his eye. "Hey, Jerry, why don't you take my R & R space? You're always going on about that nurse in San Francisco. Go visit her for Christmas."

"Great idea," I said. "But soldiers on R & R in Hawaii can't travel to the mainland, you know that."

Chuck thought about that for a moment before pointing out the obvious. "OK, so you get caught being AWOL. What's the worst thing the Army can do to you—send you to Vietnam?" He had a good point there.

Another Christmas with Donna at Uncle Joe's—the tradition won't be broken! I thought to myself. I immediately accepted his ticket. *Hawaii, here I come! And after that...I sure hoped the Army wouldn't notice...*

Arriving in Hawaii, I sat through an orientation at the military recreation center in downtown Honolulu. The presenter warned us all about the serious consequences for any soldier who tried to go to the mainland. I listened closely, and then caught a cab back to the airport and approached the Pan Am ticket counter. The agent was a young man about my age.

"A round-trip ticket at the military discount rate to San Francisco, please," I said.

"Can I please see your military orders, sir?" he replied.

Since I didn't have enough money to purchase a civilian rate ticket, I began with the story I had invented on the long flight from Vietnam.

"I understand the policy," I said, "but I have a wife and four kids in San Francisco, and I can't afford to bring them to Hawaii. I was hoping to be home for Christmas. It would mean so much to the children."

The agent paused, looked at the decorations I was wearing, and silently printed the ticket. He handed me the ticket, smiled, and said, "Enjoy Christmas with your family, Captain."

***

"Hi, Donna."

"Jerry?"

"Yes."

"Where are you?"

"At the San Francisco airport."

"What? San Francisco? How? I thought you weren't coming home until April."

"I wanted to see you and to keep the Christmas tradition of going to Uncle Joe's unbroken, so I went AWOL. I thought I would surprise you." Yes, she certainly was surprised.

***

We arrived in Fresno on Christmas Eve day. My family and friends and Donna's family were, of course, surprised and happy to see me. Being at Uncle Joe's for the family gathering was especially joyous for me. My three days at home were a blur of invitations, parties and holiday meals that I will always remember.

Joy, even Christmas joy, does not last long. After three days of festivities, the return to war was approaching quickly. Donna had to go back to work in San Francisco and I had to catch a flight to Hawaii without the authorities becoming aware of my unauthorized trip to California. Thankfully, I managed to once again slip onto a Hawaii-bound plane without incident, and from there headed back to Southeast Asia.

As I settled into my seat for the flight from Hawaii to Vietnam, I reflected on reaching the goal I had set for myself before I died. I had seen her smile, heard her voice and held her hand. Even better, I began to detect hints that Donna had, five years after my proposal, made up her mind to accept. As she dropped me at the airport, I noticed a tear slowly moving down her cheek as we said goodbye.

I managed to survive my final months in Vietnam. Donna and I were married soon after I returned home, and after forty-two years together, she remains the young lady whose long dark hair, soft voice, warm smile and mischievously sparkling eyes inspired a young soldier's secret Christmas journey home.

THE QUIET MAN

MARGARET H. SCANLON

I was facing Christmas alone for the third time. It had now been three years since my beloved husband, Dan, passed away. He and I loved the holidays and I had tried hard on my own to continue our traditions. I put up a real tree, built the miniature village underneath it and put the tiny train together. I baked all the family specialties and invited the children over for dinner—but it wasn't the same. It never will be.

We raised a large family together—three girls and five boys. And those eight children have now given me fifteen grandchildren. So a large crowd gathers at my house every year for the holidays and they all miss their "Papa's" presence just as much as I do.

That year, as usual, I attended the midnight mass at our parish church. The mass was, in fact, dedicated to my late husband, a bittersweet tribute and one that made me feel his absence all the more. Sitting in the smooth, wooden pew, I felt the music of the carols and the words of the sermon wash over me as my thoughts roamed back over my years with Dan.

We always called him the Quiet Man, a man more given to gestures than words. And his gestures over the years had been memorable—a bouquet of flowers for no particular reason; small gifts that would quietly appear at the breakfast table. My favorite surprise was the evening he came up behind me and slipped a small diamond necklace around my neck. "Just a little something to make up for the bad times," he said as he fastened it in place. Oh, he could make me smile, that husband of mine.

Even after his death, it sometimes seemed that he was still with me. The first Christmas without him was the hardest. At least it was until he made me smile. How did he do it? As I drove home from church that day, consumed by my new loss, I decided that a little Christmas music might distract me. I punched the button on the radio and settled back, expecting to hear "Silent Night" or "Angels We Have Heard on High," the typical Christmas Day fare. What came softly over the airwaves was Andy Williams's rendition of "Danny Boy," a strange selection for Christmas Day. It was a cheer-up gesture from Dan, I'm certain of it. And it made me smile.

Sensing my sadness after the special midnight mass ended, one of my grandsons offered to come home and spend the night with me. I thanked him but decided instead to spend Christmas Eve alone with my thoughts. I went home to my gaily decorated–but–empty house and settled in comfortably by a cozy fire. One by one I read the lovely holiday cards and messages I had received. Instead of the sadness I'd felt on earlier Christmases, I had a feeling of peace. Before turning in that night, I quietly thanked God for all forty-six years that Dan and I had together.

Christmas morning dawned, and I set about preparing the house for the arrival of my family. My first task was to clean out the fireplace and lay a fresh fire. This had always been Dan's favorite job; he took particular care to build a long-lasting fire, with the logs and kindling placed just so. I tried to take the same care, scraping out the burned chunk of wood from my fire the night before and sweeping out the ashes before setting the wood and kindling inside. I would wait to light it until the children and grandchildren began to arrive.

My daughter Ginny was the first to appear. She cooked up a sumptuous breakfast of scrambled eggs, bacon, toast, rolls and freshly ground coffee. I put our holiday ham in the oven and sat down to enjoy this early-morning feast with her.

As we began to eat, Ginny said, "Gee, Ma, that's a great fire you built."

"Fire?" I asked. "What fire? I haven't started it yet. It's for later this afternoon."

"Well, turn around and look," Ginny urged. And turn around I did. There was the most beautiful fire blazing away in my fireplace, a fire that I hadn't struck a match to. It was one of Dan's fires.

My daughter and I sat together in the kitchen, marveling at the scene before us. Once again, it seemed the Quiet Man was watching out for us, showing us with one of his small gestures that he was nearby and thinking of us. The warmth of the fire that year helped me melt away more of the sadness that my family still felt about the loss of their father. For now we knew that as lonely as we were without him, he was trying to let us know that we were still in his heart.

THE CHRISTMAS THAT ALMOST WASN'T

KATHRYN CANAN

"And cancel Christmas!"

This line, snarled by the Sheriff of Nottingham, is the only line I remember from the movie *Robin Hood: Prince of Thieves*. For years now I've been tempted to cancel Christmas myself.

I'm not sure when I became a grinch. Certainly I remember the magic when my children were small—tackling an elaborate gingerbread house, staying up half the night assembling bikes and writing letters from Father Christmas. I had the energy and time to crochet, cross-stitch and do needlepoint on Christmas ornaments and stockings, send personal, handwritten cards, and make or buy the perfect gifts. As an early music specialist, I delighted in discovering medieval and Renaissance Christmas music never heard in the malls, and I loved sharing this ancient music in any performances I could arrange.

Family recipes from both sides melded together to become our own traditions. Spritz and sugar cookies, almond crescents, nut butter snowballs, gingersnaps and homemade fudge were all essential. When my parents visited, they brought Springerles from our German heritage; these never caught on with the rest of my family, but I appreciated the ritual of dipping the rock-hard anise bricks with quaint pictures into coffee. Christmas breakfast had to include homemade sourdough cherry rose rolls and the oranges from our stockings, and dinner, where I resisted a menu set in stone, still had to include Yorkshire pudding and strawberry Jell-O with crushed pineapple.

The handmade stockings became the hallmark of our Christmases. They weren't just for the kids; Dave and I had them, too, and filled them for each other. As we all grew older, they took on themes. Last Christmas our younger son, Tim, on the path to becoming a cardiologist, got a bacon-themed stocking, including a tie he could wear under his white coat. Guests got them, too; when my sister Patricia visited us in California for the first time, I crocheted her a stocking and filled it with California avocados and kiwis. Trouble was, the stocking kept stretching as I added weight to it, and it morphed into the legendary Avocado Monster.

I think now that I was a victim of my own success. The problem with creating so many heartwarming Christmas traditions is that my family grew to love them—all of them. Some things need to change as children grow up and the family changes, but Christmas traditions are not conducive to change. It seemed to me, as the years went by, that the Martha Stewart Christmas I always tried to create morphed into National Lampoon's *Christmas Vacation*, with nearly as many disasters.

Now that my children are grown, they are home for only a few days during the holidays. I don't want them to waste that time shopping; I want to spend time together. One year I took my two sons skiing the day after Christmas. It was the only day that week the weather was perfect, and as we headed up to the Sierras, we felt as if we were driving into a Christmas card. We arrived at the hill by 10:00 a.m. and managed to find a parking place within two miles of the lift. Tim and I had our own equipment; Jon, who had flown down from Seattle, needed to stand in the rental line—he didn't receive his skis until 2:00 p.m. Then he had to stand in another line to trade his full-day pass for a half-day pass. We don't go skiing during Christmas week anymore.

Gifts for our children now have to fit in carry-on luggage. We avoid the problem somewhat by giving gift cards and finding new ways to wrap receipts for gifts shipped directly to their homes—creating strange ways to use paper bags and duct tape is another tradition—but it's hard to evoke the same magic on Christmas morning these days. In fact, I increasingly resist the whole commercial aspect of Christmas. I avoid the malls and make a spiritual practice out of not shopping on Black Friday.

As a musician, I'm sensitive to noise—including bad Christmas music, which starts before Halloween these days. Even my initial enthusiasm for unusual medieval and Renaissance carols has dimmed. (Must we play "Ríu Ríu Chíu" again? The tenors never come in on time.) The last time my consort played for a party at a winery in a replicated castle, we had to fend off grapes shot from spoons the guests had turned into mini-catapults. Christmas spirits can be a problem in the entertainment world.

Our daughter, Robin, became an accomplished pastry chef by the time she was twelve. She began to concoct amazing variations on everything in the cookie cookbooks we owned. Of course, we couldn't do without the traditional favorites, so we kept adding to the cookie repertoire. I bought a freezer, donated freely to every December gathering I attended and invested in cute tins for gifts of baked goods. I did compromise and get rid of the Springerles the year that rats found the dough chilling in the attic because the refrigerator was too full. I still had to get out the low-carb vegan cookbook every January to recover from the sugar high.

On Christmas Eve, Dave and I used to be able to cook and clean up dinner, go to a candlelight service, visit the Grinch and set visions of sugar plums dancing, put the kids to bed with a lullaby of Kermit singing carols with John Denver, assemble half a dozen toys, fill the stockings, arrange the presents under the tree, compose a letter from Father Christmas à la J.R.R. Tolkien for the mantel, fall into bed around 3:00 a.m., and still wake up early enough to make the cherry rose rolls before the kids clattered downstairs to the stockings. As the kids (and we) got older, it helped that they slept in longer and Father Christmas wrote his final letter to them, but the toys got more complicated, the assembly instructions were outsourced overseas and somehow we lost the ability to stay up past ten. And church? We got tired of hot wax burning our fingers while we forgot the words to "Silent Night."

The crowning glory of our Christmas disasters, however, has been the perpetual tree argument. We don't have a fake tree, and we never will. When we first moved into our house with cathedral ceilings, we happily trooped up to the foothills and brought a fifteen-foot tree home on the roof of our minivan. There were a few problems—most stands are made for eight-foot trees, and we had to accept that the topmost string of lights would always fail within a day. It got harder when we traded in the van for a Honda Civic, but we made do: we paid a high school boy with a pickup truck to deliver it, borrowed or rented a truck or bribed a neighbor with a bottle of wine (he didn't want a tin of cookies). We put the tradition on hold for a couple of years when the tree nearly fell on Robin as a toddler, but when she got old enough to dodge a potential accident the monster trees resumed.

And then we got Psycho Cat. We'd had a cat before, a nice, benign cat that knew how to go outside when necessary and was pretty laid-back about everything. He liked to sleep under the tree, and even the lowest ornaments were safe. But after Frodo died, we picked out an orphaned kitten, a calico Manx who was easily frightened and hated change. Bringing a fifteen-foot tree into the living room and covering it with lights and ornaments was change. She also never learned the difference between a throw rug and a litter box, or the difference between a Christmas tree skirt and a throw rug (please apply the transitive property of equality here).

One year, it seemed that all of the negative aspects of Christmas hit at once. Jon had married our beloved new daughter-in-law, Ramona, in August, and we had enjoyed Thanksgiving with them.

But it was her parents' turn for Christmas and they were in Denver, a thousand miles away. Dave's father, James, had died in September, and we were still deeply grieving. My Civic had been rear-ended, leaving my back and neck temporarily sore. Tim, now in medical school, was rarely awake during the few days he was home. The recession had hit, and since music lessons and live music are expendable expenses, I had no income that month. I was feeling especially anticommercial anyway; I even dragged my husband to a workshop on simplifying Christmas, but the workshop only accentuated our irreconcilable differences about the holidays. We loaded up the credit card anyway, put up the insanely tall tree and tried to keep Psycho Cat out of the living room.

Christmas came and went despite the gloom, and on December 28 Dave and I awoke to celebrate our thirtieth anniversary. We took our coffee into the living room for a peaceful, romantic morning alone, but another smell was fighting with the odors of pine and cinnamon. I threw the tree skirt into the washer and began to clean up the rest of the mess. I had to lift up the plastic mat we had placed under the tree to protect the floor, and suddenly we had a much bigger mess to deal with. Fortunately all those crocheted and embroidered ornaments weren't breakable, and the tree missed the lamps on its way down.

Just when I felt the whole season deserved to be swept under the rug, Robin came running down the stairs, several hours before she usually got out of bed during vacation. She waved her cell phone at us. "Jon says to check the porch for a package!"

She opened the door, and there stood Jon and Ramona.

Sometime in the middle of all the hugs, Jon explained, "We're spending New Year's Eve with friends in San Francisco, so we came a couple of days early to celebrate with you. Happy Anniversary!"

The newlyweds were glowing with the joy of their first Christmas as a couple, and their love transported us back to the early years of our marriage. We remembered our tiny Chicago apartment, and our first Christmas away from our families in Montana. We'd bought a small, dangerously dry tree in a drab city parking lot and covered it with generic ornaments from Woolworths. A thunderstorm on Christmas Eve destroyed any hope of a white Christmas; without a car, we splashed through the streets and shivered through a service in an unfamiliar church. And yet, that first Christmas, we also had our new baby son, whose eyes were glued to the sparkling lights. Jon was happy just playing with boxes and ribbons and getting his first taste of solid food. Now, with our family together again, welcoming Jon's new wife into our traditions, Dave and I realized that all of the "disasters" from thirty years of Christmas had transformed into good stories, a tapestry of shared memories that hold us together.

Since then, Christmas has regained its magic. We replaced the Civic with a small SUV that can carry a twelve-foot tree, and we gave three boxes worth of ornaments to our children for their own trees. I plan to make a new tree skirt in memory of Psycho Cat as soon as I finish cross-stitching Ramona's stocking. Robin's culinary experiments have expanded beyond dessert, so I have ceded control of the kitchen to her. We cut down on the cookies so we can enjoy Grandpa's favorite rum and orange juice with our adult children; we also treasure even more the time we still have with our mothers. We haven't yet missed a Christmas with the new doctor in the family, which has to be a miracle, and we've adjusted to the rhythm of sharing Jon and Ramona with her delightful parents. We're beginning to look forward to assembling toys and writing Father Christmas letters for as yet mythical grandchildren. When they do arrive, Christmas will move to their house, where they have room for a twenty-foot tree.

I'll bring the Springerles.

THE CHRISTMAS TREE

NEVA J. HODGES

What had I done? The forever vows my husband and I exchanged in a wedding ceremony a few hours ago took on a new meaning. Changing from my travel clothes into my wedding nightgown on what I'd always believed would be the most romantic night of my life, the calm and sure belief that Jim was my true love deserted me. There was so much I didn't know about love and marriage. I looked around the small motel room. And romance? When would that start on this honeymoon?

Both Jim and I were raised in a strict religious environment, and even though the sexual revolution of the sixties pervaded our culture, we waited for our wedding night to consummate our relationship. However, stolen kisses and deep caresses highlighted our dates.

Jim proposed in June 1966, when he stopped to see me at my parents' home in Pueblo, Colorado, on his way to a six-week geology field camp. That same day, he said, "Let's look at rings." I couldn't believe it. We drove downtown and walked into a jewelry store. Jim told the owner I could have whatever I wanted. A simple one suited me. It had a quarter-carat diamond set in a half loop of gold. Jim later told me he was afraid I would choose the most expensive ring in the store. My taste fit his budget, though. Then Jim told the storeowner he didn't have the money and that he was a college student. I held my breath. "No problem," the owner said. "You can make monthly payments."

In the car, Jim slid the ring onto my finger and pledged his love to me.

After he left to meet his fellow geologists in Utah, I dreamed of a June wedding a year later—time enough to save money and plan the details. My parents could not afford to pay for the wedding. I left my hometown to look for work near Jim's college in Golden, Colorado. I stayed with a friend until I had a job and enough money for rent.

I searched for a place to live and found a small in-law unit at the back of the landlord's house. At least it was private. My fiancé, though, upped the ante. He wanted the wedding during his semester break. I told him I needed time to plan. His persuasive powers carried the day. He was practical and said, "I'll have a new job after graduation and I don't want to move and get married the same month."

We chose December 23 for our wedding. Young and in love, we didn't consider that people might have other plans for the Christmas holiday. Each week before we married, Jim stopped by the little house we would soon call home and gave me a greeting card. I loved seeing him, but the cards disappointed me. They were humorous. I wanted the romantic, serious ones that pledged undying love. The words didn't match the passion we experienced every time we met. I wanted more.

I proceeded to plan our wedding, which was less than four months away, even though I worried that we were missing the romance I wanted. Many weekends I rode the bus from Denver to Pueblo, my hometown, two hours away, to choose my wedding dress, arrange for a photographer, secure my attendants and buy the cloth and patterns for their dresses. I lived paycheck to paycheck and bought less food to save money for the wedding expenses. By the time I bought my gown, I was a size eight, from a twelve. Even though I was hungry at times, my wedding dominated all that I did. A coworker saw how thin I had become and said, "Are you eating?"

I assured him I was.

The night of the rehearsal arrived. I was fine until Jim and his groomsmen teased me, laughed and in general had a good time. Tense and serious, I said, "Knock it off, you have to pay attention." They laughed, which added to my angst. I wanted a perfect wedding and, therefore, I needed a perfect rehearsal.

During the confusion, one of Jim's brothers slipped out and came back with hamburgers for everyone. It suddenly dawned on me. My fiancé hadn't planned a rehearsal dinner. Some people had driven two hours to get there and were returning home that night. They would come again the next evening for the wedding. My future husband hadn't read the bride magazines, and I later learned that he didn't know what his responsibilities were, except for choosing the groomsmen and arranging for the honeymoon.

Calm overtook me by the next morning. I rested in the afternoon and anticipated what it would feel like to have Jim make love to me that night.

Incorporating the beautiful colors of Christmas for my wedding, my attendants wore empire waist dresses, which matched the style of my white wedding dress. Their bodices were deep pink satin and the long flowing velvet skirts were deep rose. Fragrant with evergreen sprays, the floral baskets held a mix of carnations the color of the bridesmaids dresses. The containers sat on pedestals next to the white arch under which we were married. Everything went well during the ceremony until the moment we faced each other and listened to our vocalist sing "More." As the song filled the church sanctuary, I felt Jim sway—was he about to faint? I held his hands tight and pulled him closer to me. "Don't faint," I whispered. He unlocked his knees and the moment passed. Relieved, I turned my attention back to the ceremony. We said the vows we had memorized and waited for the final sentence, "You may kiss the bride." And now, to the honeymoon, the moment I'd longed for these past few months.

We drove to Colorado Springs for our first night, fooling the guests who had decorated Jim's '58 Chevrolet with cans that dangled and rattled and the words "Just Married" written in shaving cream on the rear window. We took his parents' car instead for our trip to explore the snow-covered Colorado Rockies. Yes, I did overcome my wedding night jitters, all doubts fled. But another problem soon troubled me. All the time we'd been planning this wedding, it never occurred to me to plan something for Christmas. I'd been so focused on dresses and flowers and vows. How would we celebrate our first holiday in a sterile motel? I turned to Jim that morning and admitted my mistake.

He looked at me and smiled. "I'll be right back," he said, closing the door to our room behind him. Another funny greeting card, I guessed, watching him from the window as he headed to the car. The romantic atmosphere of our wedding ceremony seemed to have faded quickly.

I guessed wrong. Jim opened the door to the room and dragged in a four-foot-tall, undecorated Christmas tree. "Merry Christmas. I put this in the trunk and thought we'd take this along with us on our trip. That way we can put it in our room every night." My husband. He was a romantic, after all. Who needed sentimental cards when the man I married could surprise me with a special gift? And after forty-six years together, he surprises me still.

Enchiladas, Hold the Beer

PAM WALTERS

Holidays are a time for nostalgia, merriment and good cheer. We clink glasses and remember the past. We salute the present. And we toast each other for happiness and good fortune in the new year. But here's a sobering thought. How many people are merely putting on a party face? While most folks are wishing for lavish presents under the tree, some people are simply wishing for a way out of their emotional pain. To many people, a certain kind of personal freedom would be the most loving gift they could give to themselves.

By the time I was eighteen, I was drinking excessively. It started innocently enough in high school, yet I already knew that drinking meant more to me than it did to my friends as we snuck booze from our parents' liquor cabinets and shared it in the back of someone's car. I behaved differently than they did when it came to liquor, and I knew that my friends thought I was beginning to have a problem as well. I could tell by the looks they gave each other when I wanted to keep drinking after everyone else had stopped. As the years went by, my dependence on alcohol increased, and by the time I was forty, alcohol wasn't just important to me, it was the only thing that mattered. I was head over heels in love, having a long-term romance with alcohol.

The day my world came apart, and the day it came together, was the day after Thanksgiving in 1989. It was my personal "black Friday," the day I hit bottom.

Thanksgiving had been just another miserable holiday for me. I spent it alone, holed up in my fancy condo on the north side of Chicago. I sat in my comfy white chair—a big tumbler of vodka in hand—overlooking Lake Michigan. It was only 2:30 in the afternoon, and I was already far too drunk. I was a daily, maintenance drinker by then and—although I started drinking in the morning—I usually paced myself so that I wouldn't pass out until around 9 p.m. But not this day. I had totally overshot my mark. What was I going to do? I couldn't stop drinking; I couldn't even slow down. And if I had a couple more, I'd surely pass out in the chair. Somehow the idea of passing out in the middle of the day was horrific. I knew I was a bad drunk, but not *that* bad.

And then something happened. Some people call it a moment of clarity. But right then, I knew the jig was up. My life passed before my eyes. I sped through the years of hopping from one advertising agency job to another—a jump ahead of getting fired for lack of performance, lack of attendance or lack of anything resembling a good attitude toward my coworkers, my bosses or the clients. I drank that promising career away, and now I was unemployed yet again.

I had never been married . . . never had any kids. I ticked off my list of unhealthy love interests that mostly centered around us getting drunk or getting high. I was estranged from my parents and other relatives. I had no girlfriends and the couple of men friends I had were only drinking buddies. And they'd pretty much given up on me, too.

I looked at all the mistakes I'd made, the harebrained schemes, the moves to different cities. Running . . . always running away from something or someone, some bad decision, the wrong job or the wrong relationship. Running away from my dysfunctional childhood. Oh, I could always drag out that old drama and try to elicit a sympathetic ear. But somehow all the running away from the truth about myself stopped and started in that white chair, in the middle of the day, the day after Thanksgiving.

I looked around my beautiful living room. Everything became slightly out of focus. I couldn't really hear the TV—my constant companion. It's as if my whole world were put on mute. I felt weightless in that chair. And I knew *this* all had to stop. I knew my entire life and everything that had happened was centered around my alcoholism; the key to me was alcohol. I faced it and, for a split second, something in me surrendered, and I opened myself up to possibilities. I whispered, "Now what?"

Suddenly the phone rang—this didn't happen often. And then someone was buzzing me from the downstairs lobby—this *never* happened. I picked up the phone. It was my old boyfriend, Tom. We were together for a couple of drunken years, and then he decided to get sober. I asked him to hold as I went to the intercom. It was a nurse I'd met at one of the AA meetings I attended as Tom's "significant other."

Between the two of them, double-teaming in an intervention, I agreed to check myself into a treatment center. As the phone calls were placed and the arrangements made, I sat in wonder that all this was unfolding in front of me, and that I was actually going along with it. Could I really break up with the bottle? Could I leave this long-term relationship behind?

Several days later, I found myself walking up the steps to a twenty-eight-day recovery center. I was still in shock at what was happening, but I kept putting one foot in front of the other and, thank God, I never turned away and bolted for the door.

The weeks passed and slowly the haze lifted. I saw myself clearly, probably for the first time in my life, but not with anguish, remorse or guilt. I saw that I was a sick person. I had a disease. Yes, I did things that were stupid and destructive, but they were knee-jerk reactions — the result of operating under the heavy cloak of alcoholism.

My life lay in front of me — blank pages yet to be filled in. I had no script, no plans and no big ideas. The day of the "big idea" was over. I was just taking it one day at a time. One revelation, one insight at a time.

And I was about to face my first sober Christmas. I was glad I was in treatment. At least I wouldn't be alone.

The administrators and counselors were dissuading us from making a big deal about Christmas. Why? Because the holiday symbolized too much nostalgia. It brought up too many emotional triggers. As a result, there were no Christmas decorations, and we weren't allowed to accept gifts or cards from the outside. For dinner Christmas Eve, we had tuna noodle casserole. Not exactly your traditional holiday fare. After dinner and a low-key group session, we each retired to our rooms.

But in the middle of the night, I was wide awake. It was Christmas, after all. A day in which gifts from the heart are given and received. How could I express the love that was developing inside me, not just for my sober self, but also for those who were helping me on this difficult journey? *There must be some way I can show them,* I thought as I quietly padded around the facility. I poked around until I hit the laundry room. There on long bars, hung up high, were dozens of my housemates' blouses, jeans and T-shirts. Bingo. I'd found it. There was a way I could put my love into action.

So at 3:30 on Christmas morning, I ironed everyone's clothes. I didn't tell them who'd done it. It was my secret gift to them.

That Christmas day was the same as all the others in that twenty-eight-day center. Morning meditation, group therapy, individual counseling and so on. And for Christmas dinner, we were served enchiladas. We all laughed and spontaneously said: "Hold the Corona."

That was twenty-three years ago. It's hard to believe; it's a miracle, actually. I never looked back, not once. I just stared straight ahead at my unknown future. One step in front of the other, one day at a time. And miracles have happened to me *beyond my wildest dreams.* Unbelievably wonderful things have occurred. I wouldn't even have dreamed to ask for what's happened; I would have shortchanged myself. But the most important gifts I've received are the gifts of freedom, serenity, peace of mind and true joy. Getting sober was the most loving Christmas present I have ever received, and yes, it came hand-delivered from me to me.

PERFECT RECORD

LELIA KUTGER, AS TOLD TO APRIL KUTGER

There was a fierce blizzard in the days before Christmas in 1951. We were snowed in in Morrisville, Pennsylvania. Snowplows had left four-foot high drifts blocking the driveway. We had our tree, but, according to tradition, would not decorate it until Christmas Eve. The presents for the girls were stowed in the trunk of my big, old Packard. It was all up to me this year, just as it had been for our daughter JoAnne's first Christmas some years before, during World War II. That was the year I got the telegram.

Joe was a navigator for the B-24 bombers dropping their payloads over Germany. I feared for his life every day, but my precious baby girl diverted my attention from missing her father. JoAnne was born in September 1944, nine months after Joe's and my first Christmas together. I hadn't seen him since that Christmas. I had sent pictures of our baby girl to Joe, but I hadn't received a letter from him since a short V-mail, bursting with joy and relief that his first child had been born safely. I wished so much that he could be with us for JoAnne's first Christmas, but it was the same for me as for most of the women I knew. The men were off at war.

It was November 30 when the boy who worked at the drugstore rode his bike up to the cottage we rented near Fort Dix, New Jersey. JoAnne was asleep in her cradle and I was folding diapers, stiff from drying in the cold air.

"Ma'am," he said with a small nod. He was holding a yellow envelope in his hand. A telegram. I sucked in my breath, but didn't make a sound. The boy pushed the envelope toward me and repeated, "Ma'am." I took it from his gloved hand and, for some absurd reason, I said, "Thank you." I handed him a quarter from my coin purse and stood in the open doorway, staring into space. It was several moments before the chill air made me realize where I was.

Clutching the telegram to my breast, I sat down on the navy-blue-velvet couch my parents had handed down to us. I couldn't open it. I went to the kitchen to reheat the morning coffee. It would taste bitter, but my mouth was already bitter. I swallowed a big gulp. Suddenly I was in a cold sweat and shaking. I ran to the bathroom and threw up. "This is absurd," I said to myself. "I don't even know what's in the telegram." But I knew. I went back to the kitchen and sat down again, slipped my thumb under the envelope flap and gently pried it open as if it were an ancient papyrus artifact.

"LT JOSEPH P KUTGER MISSING IN ACTION STOP."
I stopped.

Five months after that lonely and anxious time, not knowing if Joe was dead or alive or, as proved to be true, a prisoner of war, the war in Europe ended. A month later Joe was transferred to a stateside hospital. The following Christmas I was four months' pregnant with our second child. Joe was healthy and had gained back most of the weight he'd lost in prison camp. On Christmas Eve he gave me a gold crucifix. He told me it should remind me that I was never alone, because God was always with me. I cried and said, "It's beautiful, but I want *you* to always be with me." Joe held me in his arms and said he would never miss another Christmas. I knew he might not be able to keep that promise. But now it had been six years, and he had.

In 1951 Joe was stationed at Godman Air Field near Fort Knox, Kentucky, more than seven hundred miles from where the children and I lived. I hadn't seen him for three months, but after a lot of finagling, trading duty assignments and finishing his training assignment ahead of schedule, Joe told me he thought he would be able to make it home at least for a few days. He was going to hitch a couple of rides on puddle jumpers that would get him to Millville Air Field in New Jersey.

Then the blizzard blanketed the East Coast and another one was expected. Joe called to say, "There's no way I can get there, Honey. I'm really sorry. I wanted to keep my promise. I did everything I could to make this happen."

"Oh, Joe," I cried.

"Honey, I'm sorry. I can't help it."

"What about the girls? They've been counting down the days until you'd be here."

"You know I would if I could, but there are no flights operating. It's just not possible."

"I can't do this without you, Joe. I can't make Christmas without you."

"You have to, Lee. You have to be strong and make everything about this Christmas the same as always. Make sugar cookies. Decorate the tree on Christmas Eve. Open the presents in the morning. Serve roast beef for Christmas dinner . . ."

"Oh, Joe, I feel like I did when you were shot down in '44. I need you."

"I know you can do this, Hon. Are you wearing your crucifix? Remember, you're not alone. God is with you."

"I hate it when you tell me that whenever I'm missing you too much. I don't want God. I want you." I caught my breath and said, "Sorry. I didn't mean that. I do want God. It's just that I want you so much."

"It's going to be okay, Sweetheart."

I blew my nose and modulated my tone. "I know. I can do it. Don't worry," I told him, even though I didn't feel that way at all.

"That's my girl."

With the driveway packed in, we couldn't get to church on Sunday, and the weatherman forecasted a new storm by nightfall. I hoped my brother, Ralph, would be able to make it on Christmas Day. I always counted on Ralph to be there for me when Joe was gone.

It did not snow Sunday night, and I got my hopes up that we might be able to dig out soon. On Monday, Christmas Eve morning, a friend of Joe's showed up with a pickup truck and a plow.

"Pete," I yelled from the front door, "what are you doing here?"

"Joe called me, so here I am," he laughed. My sweet husband. Taking care of us even when he was hundreds of miles away.

"Thank you so much, Pete."

"I'm happy to do it, Lee."

"Come on in for a cup of coffee."

"I will when I'm finished."

Pete cleared the driveway, the front steps and the walkway, as well as a path to the garage at the edge of the woods behind the house, which made it possible for us to keep one of our traditions. We always cut evergreen boughs to decorate the mantle and banister and a few to burn in the fireplace to give the house the wonderful smell of burning pine needles and the popping sound of pinecones.

A short time later, my very devoted milkman trudged through two-feet-deep snow to deliver three quarts of milk, a pound of butter and a dozen eggs. Another dilemma resolved. I had the ingredients I needed to make cookies. I handed him a Christmas card with $2 in it. Before he left, he said, "You're lucky to have power."

We had radio reception, too, so we could listen, as we did every morning, to Don McNeill's Breakfast Club. I did the dishes and the laundry, and the girls marched around the table when Don told them to. By 11:00 a.m., the sky was heavily overcast and the neighborhood was eerily silent except for the occasional sound of a tree branch breaking. The storm was on its way.

The night before I had told the girls their daddy could not come for Christmas. They were crushed, but soon they stopped crying and then whimpered into sleep as I sang to them. They had seemed fine all morning, but now I could tell they were not taking it well. They were ripping around the house like monkeys that had escaped from the zoo. Whooping and hollering. Arguing and taunting and fighting. JoAnne teased April. April cried and hit her. JoAnne ran to me to tattle. Finally, I said, "Naptime! And separate bedrooms!"

"I get Mommy's bed," JoAnne shouted.

"No, me!" April whined.

When there was silence from the second floor, I lay down, too. I slept fitfully until I heard little voices calling, "Can we get up now, Mommy?"

After peanut butter and jelly sandwiches and hot chocolate, I bundled the girls into their snowsuits. Fresh air would be good for all of us. "Come on. We're going to cut tree branches and put big red ribbons on them."

"Can I help, Mommy?" April asked with great enthusiasm.

"Of course, Honey. I want you to tell me which branches are the best."

I got my garden shears, and we tramped through the snow to the woods behind the house. It was hard for my cherubs to make their way through the deep snow, but we followed the path Pete had plowed.

"I'm cold, Mommy," my little towhead April cried after we were out for a few minutes.

"We'll go in soon, Honey."

JoAnne, my stubborn and determined girl, said, "Can't we stay out and make snow angels?" Before I could answer, the first new flurries began to fall.

As soon as we were inside, I called Ralph. "Why don't you come now? Stay overnight with us. The roads will be impossible in an hour." He was silent. "I have pork chops for dinner," I coaxed.

"I was on my way to a friend's. His parents came down for the holiday."

"Please, Ralph." I didn't want to be alone.

"Okay, Sis. Do you want me to pick anything up on the way?"

"I can't think of anything—just get here before it's too dangerous."

Ralph made it to us just as the early winter twilight fell. He scooped the girls up and threw them in the air as they screamed and giggled. I heated up my hard cider for the two of us, something Joe and I always shared on Christmas Eve.

"Thank you," I told him. "For everything." We shared a smile.

After dinner, the four of us gathered around the tree. "You girls do the low branches, I'll do the middle and Uncle Ralph will do the high ones," I announced. When we were finished, Ralph carefully placed an heirloom angel in a white satin dress on the very top branch. JoAnne and April clapped and oohed and aahed; their eyes shining with the reflection of the Christmas lights.

"And now it's time for bed, girls," I said. They were wearing matching red plaid flannel nightgowns and fluffy slippers. Joe's and my little angels.

"I wish Daddy was here," JoAnne said, tears starting to fall.

"Me, too," cried April.

I hugged my girls and said, "I wish Daddy was here, too. But we'll be okay."

"I'll take them up," Ralph said, his hands reaching out for theirs.

"Thanks, Ralph. I'm beat." I gave each little forehead a good-night kiss and leaned back on the couch.

Ralph stayed downstairs with me until midnight, and I think we both got a little tipsy. We had been listening to Christmas songs on the radio and sharing stories of our childhood. I blubbered as I told Ralph how much I missed Joe, especially at Christmas. "It's just like the war. I went more than a year without seeing him when he was a POW. At first I didn't even know if he was alive."

Ralph had heard the story many times. He always listened sympathetically, but not for too long. He started making fun of me and my tears and my memories. "You are not going to look like a merry Christmas girl with those swollen eyes and mascara running down your cheeks." I laughed and wiped my eyes. "How do you think Joe would feel if he saw you like this? It's bad enough that he can't be here, but then to think you've become completely discombobulated in his absence." Now I couldn't stop laughing. "Soused and sobbing on Christmas Eve. Or is it Christmas morning?" he said as he looked at his watch. "You're not the woman Joe married, I can tell you that. Pull yourself together, Sis!" Ralph grabbed my shoulders and shook me in jest. I was laughing so hard I thought I would wake the girls.

After Ralph climbed the stairs, I lay down on the old blue-velvet couch—Joe's favorite place to nap. I turned the radio to a station that played the Hit Parade. Everything from Johnnie Ray's "Cry" and "Too Young" by Nat King Cole to Les Paul and Mary Ford's "How High the Moon." I loved that one. Joe said he played it on the Officer's Club jukebox because it made him think of me. I couldn't help shedding a tear. I wondered if Joe was listening to it now.

As I held my "missing Joe" crucifix between my thumb and forefinger, I prayed the prayer I had repeated so often when Joe was a POW. "Keep him safe, Lord. Bring him home to me. Take care of him. Keep him warm. Let him know how much I love him. Bring him home safe and sound." As I drifted off, I imagined I smelled Joe's hair cream emanating from the doily on the couch's armrest.

Only minutes later, I woke with a start, but then lay dead still. Someone was jiggling the front doorknob. Then I heard the floor creak in the hallway. Oh, dear Lord, protect my children. My heart was pounding so hard I thought it would explode. I was afraid to breathe. A burly man walked slowly, silently, toward the center of the room where the tree lights twinkled. I didn't move. The figure turned toward me.

"Oh, my goodness! Joe!" I gasped as I jumped up.

"I promised you I would always be home for Christmas." He leaned over and kissed my forehead, then my eyelids, then my lips. "Don't cry, Honey," he said, wiping away my tears. "I only have a few hours. Let's make the most of it." He zipped himself out of his thick shearling flight suit and boots, which added twenty pounds to his frame, and sat down beside me.

"Did you make your hard cider this year?" he asked, rubbing his cold, red hands together.

"Of course." I kissed every square inch of his visible skin. "Joe, you're freezing," I said, my arms tightening around his shivering body.

"You're right. I *am* freezing, I'll tell you about it after I get my hands around a warm mug of cider."

Once he was settled and warm, Joe told me how he got home. "I borrowed a car from a pilot who couldn't leave the base. A Fiat. Tiniest car you've ever seen. Italian. Not built for snow. It had a broken heater, but I decided to go for it. I wore my flight suit to stay warm."

"But Joe, if you broke down on an empty road, you could have frozen to death."

"I was okay until I got to Pittsburgh. Then the driver's side windshield wiper broke. I had to drive with my hand out the window to clear off the snow."

Armed with nothing but a thermos of coffee, he drove for twenty straight hours, through a raging snowstorm. He was never able to go faster than 45 mph, often a lot slower. Then the car simply stopped in one of the tunnels. It was only a matter of reconnecting the alternator wire, but if there had been other cars on the road, he would have caused a pileup.

As thrilled as I was to be nestled in Joe's arms, the thought of what he had done to get home terrified me. "Joe, you shouldn't have done it. You could have gotten killed."

"When I got home from the war," Joe whispered, "I made you a promise that I'd never again leave you alone on Christmas. My record's been perfect so far. I didn't want to break it. And the look in your eyes makes it all worthwhile."

GIVING SHELTER

MELISSA CHAMBERS

It was that time of year . . . I was busy preparing for Christmas, getting the tree up and trimmed, decorating the house, shopping and
attempting to hold the attention of thirty fifth-graders for six hours
a day. It was also a time of discovery; just a few weeks before my
boyfriend had moved in, and we were still learning what that was
like. We had so much in common, Charlie and I—a love of animals,
books and political discussion. Life was wonderful, and I suspected
that he was starting to think about marriage. But . . . were we really
a perfect match? I'd made a mistake once before, so how could I be
sure I wouldn't make another one?

This holiday season, rather than donating to a local animal rescue, as I had for the last few years, I had decided to become involved in
animal rescue myself. "Great idea," Charlie had said when I told him
about my plan to drive a few hours down to the Central Valley with
Susan, a new friend who volunteered for a local rescue, and "pull"
a couple of dogs from an overcrowded shelter she'd learned about.

The plan was that we'd bring the dogs north to our town and we would have them spayed or neutered and foster them until new homes were found for each of them. It was a long drive, through areas known for thick "Tule fog" this time of year. "Getting the dogs is wonderful," he'd said, and then added, "but wait until the fog burns off before you get on the road."

***

As the day grew closer, I was more excited about our rescue mission than I was about the approaching holiday. For the last week, every evening, when I should have been wrapping presents, I had instead been looking at the dogs on the shelter's website. A few days earlier I had decided to pull an adult Chihuahua and notified the shelter of my intent, but then had received word yesterday that she had not survived a bout of kennel cough.

Lying awake in bed that last night, reviewing everything I needed to pack in the morning for the trip, I kept seeing the big, scared eyes of the little blond Chihuahua. I'd already become attached to her just by seeing her picture. I felt it was my fault that she had died. What if I had taken off work and gone down there a few days earlier? Would I have been able to save her? I'd never had an animal's death on my conscience before. As I tossed and turned, unable to quiet my thoughts enough to sleep, I realized what I would be doing tomorrow was playing God. The dogs I chose to bring back with me would be given a chance to survive. I knew that, but somehow had not con-nected the dots and realized that I would pretty much be sealing the fate of those I left behind. After that unwelcome epiphany, I didn't think I would sleep at all, but I must have succumbed at some point because I was awakened from a deep sleep by the alarm at 8:30. We planned to hit the road about 1 p.m., which left plenty of time to pack everything and for the fog to burn off.

Traffic had been heavy with holiday travelers, but luckily there was no fog. Susan called the shelter to let them know we would not be getting there until after they had closed for the day.

Our first stop once we reached the shelter was the isolation ward for sick and injured dogs. A tiny ginger-hued Chihuahua puppy with caramel eyes peered out at me from the first cage I saw. One of his front paws flopped uselessly from the joint, but that didn't stop him from plastering himself against the bars of the cage and sticking his long pink tongue out to lick my hand. A shelter worker in the room looked at his intake card and told us, "We don't have a vet here, so he'll be put down in the morning." "Oh no, he won't," I responded, lifting him from the cage and wrapping my coat around his wriggling body.

A few cages further down we saw a dog that looked like a Jack Russell Terrier, but with very short legs, that seemed to have swallowed a watermelon. Because she was pregnant, she was also scheduled for euthanasia the next day, we were told. Her tail beat the air like a metronome as she threw herself at the bars over and over in an effort to get to us. Vanessa, as her kennel card identified her, was in a crate and ready to go in moments. *Surely Charlie would understand why I couldn't leave her, wouldn't he?* I asked myself.

The main kennels were so loud that conversation was impossible. This part of the shelter had openings to small outside areas attached to each kennel, and the icy December wind rushed in. I huddled deeper in my coat and gaped at the packed kennels whose floors were wet from when they had last been washed. With no way to get off the wet floor, the dogs were huddling together in piles, trying to get warm.

I blinked tears from my eyes as I thought of Charlie and the three dogs we already owned, at home, warm and safe. This time of the evening would find them snuggled together on the living room couch, the cheerful glow from the lights of the Christmas tree in front of the window competing with the blue light of the television across the room. Our dogs each had a Christmas stocking hung from the bookcase, between Charlie's and mine. On Christmas morning they would be filled with chew toys, carrots and tiny tennis balls. At night they slept upstairs in the bed with us. Each had his or her special spot, and woe to the dog that tried to muscle in on another's territory. The dogs were all mine, but when Charlie moved in, they were ecstatic to have someone else to lavish attention on them. All had been adopted from rescues. I hoped they had forgotten that part of their lives, now that they were used to being warm and dry and fed and loved. How many of the shivering dogs surrounding me now, I wondered, would get the chance to be part of a family again? There wasn't one of them that didn't deserve to have its own stocking filled with treats to devour on Christmas morning.

At least I could make a difference in the lives of a couple of them today. Last night over dinner I had promised Charlie I would pull just one or two dogs from the shelter. Small Chihuahuas like we had at home, because the Central Valley shelters were overflowing with them. I promised him they wouldn't be any trouble. The amount of money I spent getting them spayed or neutered would be the amount I asked for their adoption fee, so they would not be a financial burden. "You will hardly know they're here before they'll be gone and in their new loving homes!" I'd insisted this afternoon as I shrugged into my coat. "Just be safe and let me know when you're heading back," Charlie replied as I gave him a quick hug and headed for the door. Now I realized that I could not keep my word. I had lied to him. At the time I had thought I could save just two dogs. I had already chosen two, and one was going to deliver puppies any day! Charlie trusted me. I knew how important honesty was in a relationship. Should I call and ask him if he would mind if I brought home more than two? Could I even leave the shelter with just these two dogs? How would he react when he found out I had broken my promise? Adding two dogs to our home, even temporarily, would be a bit stressful. More than two, more stress. What kind of reaction could I expect? Would he be angry? Feel he could no longer trust me to keep my word? Would he move out, leaving me to spend Christmas alone?

These thoughts chased around in my head as I surveyed the small faces surrounding me, begging me with their eyes, reaching for me with their tiny paws, each asking to be saved.

I texted Charlie when we left the shelter and headed back up north but didn't mention anything about the dogs I was bringing home. It was almost 1 a.m. before we made it back to Sacramento.

After dropping Susan and her new foster dogs off, I headed home, part of me eager to be back, another part wanting to delay having to face Charlie and tell him what I'd done.

The lights of our Christmas tree were still on, clearly visible through the front window as I pulled into the driveway. I wished I could leave the dogs in the car while I went in and prepared Charlie, but the night was much too cold. As I began carrying in crate after crate I told him in bits and pieces about what I had seen in the shelter: the cold wet kennels, the pleading faces of the dogs, the impossibility of saving only two. His eyes wide, Charlie listened without saying anything and eyed the growing number of crates I placed next to our Christmas tree. When the last crate was inside I stood before him, and said, "That's why I brought home eight dogs, rather than just two, as I promised." By that time the long day had caught up with me, and I was swaying on my feet. Charlie took me in his arms and wrapped me in a warm embrace. He looked down into my eyes and said, "Melissa, don't apologize. I would have brought home more." I hugged him back as hard as I could. No man could have said anything sweeter. I had made the right choice at last.

A Christmas Letter to My Wife of Fifty Years

JACK SKILLICORN

My Dearest Sandy:

It's that time of year again. You've just headed out to the store to stock up on holiday treats, and here I sit to begin the process of writing our annual holiday letter to friends and relatives. This year I am having a difficult time concentrating, though. It could be the glass of our favorite wine that I've just poured, or it could be that every few minutes I look up from the page and focus on our newly decorated Christmas tree, hung with the ornaments we've collected, homemade strings of popcorn and the golden star we use every year at the top of the tree. Yes, I know most wives don't think their husbands notice these kinds of small details but, Sandy, I do.

This holiday letter should be easy to write: after all, the formula is a well-worn one — a few paragraphs and some photos from trips *we took, family updates on the kids and grandkids, throw in a few pet stories and voilà, I'm done. Or sometimes letter writers like to reminisce about holidays past. That should be an easy one to pull off; I have memories from fifty Christmases past to draw from . . . but no, this afternoon all I can focus on is you. Us. Our life together, as symbolized by a warmly lit and glittering tree. To heck with the Christmas letter—I'll send two next year instead. This letter, Sandy, is for you.*

That gold star perched at the top of the tree? It takes me back fifty years to you, our young daughter, Jeanette, and I celebrating Christmas together for the very first time as a newly made family in Massachusetts, snow on the ground and frost on the windows. With you in my arms and smiles on our faces, we watched a five-year-old delight in her presents. It was my first moment as her father, and I remember it so clearly.

And the peacock ornaments there on the branch near the window—I know exactly where they came from and when. 1965, Thailand. You came from California to visit me when I was stationed at the Ubon Air Force Base. You arrived in Bangkok after giving me very specific instructions not to waste a day of my leave coming down from Ubon just to meet your plane. Instructions I, of course, ignored! Watching you walk off the plane and seeing the look on your happy face when you saw that I had ignored your instructions was worth it. Holding you there in the airport wasn't half bad, either. The blue, red and yellow cloth peacock ornaments are from a local marketplace in Ubon. I remember you wrapping each one to put in your suitcase when your visit ended all too soon. More than fifty years later, the colors are still vibrant, and so is my memory of you in that moment.

The small brass photo ornament in the middle of the tree, that is from 1968 in California. Our daughter Margaret was only three months old that Christmas. Is there ever a better present under the tree than a newborn baby in a red-velvet jumper and a white blouse with a lace collar and a Santa cap?

That clear glass ornament up there, near the top of the tree, filled with sand and seashells? Of course it is from 1979 in Maui. Moonlight walks on the beach, just the two of us walking hand in hand through the surf. What a trip—it is no wonder that we try to go back as often as we can.

I could go on and on, through each of the ornaments that we pull out of the box every year, dust off and then hang together as Christmas music plays in the background and the smell of baking cookies wafts in from the kitchen.

And now here we are, in our fiftieth year together. Such amazing memories, yes, but even more amazing will be the happy times and continuing romance in the coming years. Who knew, so many years ago, that it would turn out this well? I did, Sandy. I knew. I knew it when we bought that gold star, when we first held our children together, when we walked on beach after beach. Day in and day out, I knew. Christmas only comes once a year, but our long romance is never ending.

Your husband,

Jack

THE CRUMPLED CARD

JULAINA KLEIST-CORWIN

The cold December Saturday amplified the chill in my body. I raised the thermostat in my San Francisco Bay home, and the heater roared warmth. But it didn't help. I paced in circles around my luggage and in straight lines down the hall. The shiver of anxiety wouldn't stop. I expected a phone call from Mitchell at any moment.

We had attended a health conference in Paris, and it had been a romantic trip, blended with business. When we returned to the airport's extended-stay parking lot, we kissed. Then he opened the door to my Nissan. I entered and rolled down the window. He kissed me again before he walked to his car nearby. We waved goodbye through our car windows and drove our separate ways.

No sooner had I arrived home that afternoon then I dropped my bags and raced to the phone to check for messages, expecting to have already heard from him. Nothing. No message. Nothing then, and nothing in the days since. Had he already forgotten our two weeks together in the dreamiest city in the world? My bags still sat there on the rug where I'd left them. Still packed and unattended. In the time I'd been home I still hadn't had the heart to open them and face the reminders of Paris and, him.

This had to stop. I called my mother to come over and help me unpack. The doorbell rang, we hugged at the door and I offered her a cup of coffee.

"No, thanks. It's too hot in here." She took off her white Christmas-decorated sweater and pushed up the sleeves of her turtleneck. In winter, she always wore monochromatic navy-blue clothes, except for a few white holiday tops. I turned down the thermostat. No need for heat when my mom always brightened the cloud of gloom. We both knew I was capable of unpacking one bulging suitcase and a small carry-on by myself, but she didn't question me. She could recognize a distraught daughter and would stay calm until I explained. I opened my luggage and dug among my now-wrinkled clothes to find the souvenir of the Eiffel Tower I had brought back for her. I skirted the topic of Mitchell by asking what she had done during the time I was gone.

She summarized two weeks in two minutes and then nudged my elbow. "So, tell me, what did you do together? Did you sightsee with Mitchell, or did you have to go on guided tours with the conference group?"

Of course, she actually wanted to know if Mitchell and I had made commitments. Her mantra the last few months repeated in my head, "Divorced for three years, it's time you settle down with a good man." She was right. I was ready. Best of all, I had found Mitchell.

The day we met less than a year ago, I fell in love with him. I thought that by now he cared for me in the same way.

"We went with the group to the Louvre, the Arc de Triomphe, Montmartre and Notre Dame." I didn't tell her we'd ditched the group at the cathedral in the late afternoon and had the best time finding a picturesque restaurant for dinner. I also left out the part about the boat trip on the Seine to see the lights on the Eiffel Tower.

I brought the lightweight laundry basket closer to us. She had her arms folded; her patience with me clearly dwindling fast. Tilting her head to one side, she raised her eyebrows with a silent question. I shrugged in a silent response. "Am I keeping you in suspense?" Two pairs of folded jeans remained in the suitcase, which I picked up and held to my heart. "I bought these on the Champs-Élysées. Oh, I do love Paris."

"Loving a city is different than loving a man." Her voice had a discouraged tone, and she shook her head. I had dumped my suitcases' contents on the bed, and she sorted the blouses into hand-wash and machine-wash piles.

"Being in Paris together confirmed how I feel." My eyes welled up from the worry that maybe something had gone wrong on his end. What could it be? I grabbed my travel-sized cosmetics bag and went to return the items to the adjoining bathroom. I didn't want my mother to see me cry.

I talked louder from there, so she could hear me. "Mitchell and I had a day and evening to ourselves. We went to the Musée d'Orsay to see many of the French Impressionist paintings I've studied and admired for years. They were awesome. Then we took the speed train to visit one of his colleagues who served us dinner at his home in Vendôme. The family didn't speak English, but we managed to communicate with pantomime." I didn't tell her how I'd cried bittersweet tears in the restroom on the train back to Paris. We would fly home the next day, and I didn't want the trip to end.

I carried the empty suitcases to the garage door. I was also carrying an empty heart. "I'll put 'em away later. Thanks for your help. It would have been a lot sadder to unpack by myself."

She put her hand on my forearm. "Sad? But, Honey, I thought you had a romantic trip."

"I did. It felt like a honeymoon. But he hasn't called at all since we got back. Maybe, for him, it was just a fling." I plopped onto the living room love seat, and my mother took a seat on the wicker chair, her lips pressed together in a tight line.

The look on her face made me crumple inside and brought my sobs to the surface. She got up and wrapped her arms around me, comforting me as only a mother can. "Maybe he's busy at work. Maybe he had to catch up after being out of town."

I had thought of that, too, but even busy people have time to text. "I thought I'd send him a Christmas card, but he's Jewish and I don't want to make a religious mistake."

"A card? Why not just call him yourself?"

"Never. I have to know that he wants to be with me. I wouldn't want him to see me again just to humor me or to feel as if he has to make up an excuse not to see me again."

We ate chocolate ice cream, and I shared more stories about the Parisian places I'd visited. When she left, I pulled the blank Hanukkah card I'd bought out of my purse. Yes, I had already bought him a card for his upcoming holiday. It was generic and distant. Not something I'd give to a man I wanted to marry. I signed my name without love or best wishes, just my signature, and I wrote his address on the envelope.

I didn't mail it, though. The card stayed in my purse, the envelope bending and the corners crumpling more each day. I couldn't bring myself to drop it into the mailbox. Work wasn't enough of a distraction for me. Flashes of scenes from Paris kept popping up, and I missed Mitchell more than I would ever have guessed. I wrote out Christmas cards to my friends and family and mailed them all, but still the Hanukkah card withered in my purse.

Ten nights passed without a word. That night I brought out my tabletop artificial Christmas tree. I turned off the house lights after 8 p.m. and stared at the twinkling clear bulbs wrapped around the branches, imagining the tree to be the Eiffel Tower. I remembered the hum of the boat's motor as we glided on the smooth river. Mitchell had wrapped his strong arms around me as the sparkling tower came into view in the distance. We floated closer to the magical lights, and I put my head on his shoulder. He kissed my forehead several times. When we reached the tower in all its brilliance, we embraced, and I was sure a lightning bolt of energy connected us.

I must have been wrong. Ten days after that magical moment, I was alone in my house with a twinkling fake tree.

The next day I shuffled through a mall in a throng of excited shoppers. There were a few Christmas gifts I needed to buy for friends and family. I carefully avoided the men's section at Macy's. I looked away when I passed display windows filled with glittery engagement rings.

Dumping my packages on the kitchen table, I went straight to the bathroom to run a hot tub. My day was done. A bath and an early bedtime—that was all I had to look forward to. The phone rang at about 6:30 p.m. I wrapped my pink terrycloth robe around me and reached to answer it.

Mitchell's voice greeted me. "Are you ready to celebrate the holiday tonight?"

What? He sounded like I was supposed to be remembering a prearranged date. My heart pounded. "Tonight?"

"Did you forget? Remember I said I wouldn't be able to see you for a while but that we'd have dinner on Hanukkah?"

No, I didn't remember him saying that. I certainly would have remembered. Nevertheless, he sounded sincere; maybe he thought he had told me. I stifled my surprise with the first thought that came to mind. "I guess I didn't realize Hanukkah started tonight." Since returning from Europe, though, I had marked the days on my wall calendar. I knew the Jewish holiday had arrived, and I had been ready to toss that Hanukkah card in the trash.

An hour later, we met at the Holy Land Restaurant on College Avenue in Berkeley. He gave me a tight hug and seemed happy to see me. This was the man who hadn't called? It didn't seem possible, but yet... We chatted about Paris and work, ordered matzo ball soup and falafel. When we finished our meal, Mitchell reached for my hand and his deep brown eyes teased me as if he had a surprise. Then he pulled out a present from his pocket and put it into my hand, with an expression that chased away all my doubts. "Happy Hanukkah, Julaina."

I mumbled a thank-you. My face burned with embarrassment. "Um, I have this card for you, but, um, it's not in very good shape. I've carried it around for days." I retrieved it from my purse and placed it on his side of the table.

He smiled and nodded toward the gift he had given to me. The wrapping paper had the Star of David on it. I took his nod to mean I should open it. I struggled with the ribbon and tape on the five-inch-square box. When I opened it, I gasped. A multistring necklace of small jade beads lay on a bed of cotton.

"It was made in Israel." He shifted in his chair. "I worried it wouldn't arrive in time. I didn't want to spoil the surprise, and I knew I would tell you about it if I talked to you before tonight. It was a long wait. Eleven days were too long without you."

From across the table I nodded numbly, fingering the beautiful necklace.

He opened the envelope I had brought, acted like there were no bent corners, and read it. His face beamed, but I wondered how a card could compare to the treasured necklace.

Mitchell rose from his chair and came around behind me, gently clasping the strings of Israeli jade around my neck. This precious gift was the first of many necklaces he gave me for every holiday that came along. On my birthday that year, he gave me an engagement ring and a year later, we were married. I found gifts for him, too, but I've never given him another Hanukkah card.

We celebrate two holidays every December. I plug in my tabletop Christmas tree, and he lights the candles on the menorah. We share my pretense that the tree is the Eiffel Tower, and he says the flames on the menorah's candles represent the love we have for each other. And the best part about being married to Mitchell? He's never kept me waiting again.

A Box of Memories

CHRISTINA RICHTER

We had passed the seven-year itch, but it was looking as if we might hit the ten-year ditch. My husband and I were both working full-time, juggling kids and family responsibilities, leaving no time for romance—let alone a nice discussion once in a while. Christmas was coming, which meant yet another activity was added to our already full lives.

Even though we were busy, little girls have a way with their fathers, and our daughters were no exception. Audrey and Anna, six and four, were especially fond of their papa, and he was completely smitten. Whenever they were together, the three of them would talk endlessly. But I noticed lately their chatter occurred only when I wasn't in the room. I knew they were up to something!

Secrets were not easily kept as we lived in a very small house back then. The little one-bedroom post-WWII bungalow was advertised at 1,200 square feet, but in reality it was barely that size. It had a cute front room with '40s-style casement windows, a tiny dining room attached to a galley kitchen and a walk-through room to the back porch that you might call a den. The spot dubbed as the laundry room only had space for a washing machine, so our dryer had to service us from the back patio.

The house didn't afford much privacy, but there was one place that was entirely the domain of my husband—the garage. It was actually quite spacious for the size of house, and Mark set up his office in its confines. Not that he needed an office; he just needed his space. I didn't venture into that area much; among other things, I was too busy with a full-time job and being an involved mother of two active daughters to notice what happened in the garage. In fact, it usually came as a relief when he and the girls were occupied in "Hubby's office."

The fall of 1996 was rather chilly in Southern California, so the garage door remained closed much of the time. I noticed around Halloween that the three of them were behind that door more than usual. The day I knocked and asked to come in was the day I was certain they were scheming something. All three of them responded, "You can't come in!" I knew better than to ask why, so I announced that dinner would be ready soon and walked away.

They sat down at the table full of giggles. These three had a secret and, judging by their dad's face, they weren't about to give up many clues. "What are you up to?" I asked very pointedly to the older of the two.

Audrey looked at her sister. "Noooothing!" Knowing I might get something out of them if I pressed, their dad quickly changed the subject. Dinner proceeded as usual and the subject was easily lost in the chaos of everyday life.

Before I knew it, Christmas was just days away. It seemed my job was demanding more of me than usual, but it could have just been the life of a full-time working mom at the holidays. Report deadlines, school parties, holiday cards, Christmas gifts and tree trimming all added up, and the days flew by.

I had no idea what to get my husband that year. He was just as busy as I was, so we hadn't really discussed gifts. At the last minute I settled on some clothes and a few other meaningless items. I didn't even think about feeling guilty. I was just getting through this year by crossing things off the to-do list. The presents were purchased, wrapped and under the tree. Check. I was ready.

Christmas morning is by far one of the best times for memories in our family. Glittering decorations complete with a tree filled with homemade ornaments, Christmas music and an aromatic breakfast in the oven provide the setting. Our excited eagerness and laughter provide the memories. As we gathered that December 25, it was no different. The girls and their father were especially full of smiles that morning.

Gift giving proceeded as usual. Noisy tears of wrapping paper, squeals of delight and appreciative, loving hugs filled our morning. The last present under the tree had finally been opened and the girls looked at their father in anticipation. Did he really forget to get a gift for me this year?

He looked at me and asked the girls if they were ready. In unison they replied, "Yes!" They grabbed my hands, made me close my eyes and led me out the front door. I heard the garage door opening and a quick shuffling. As I stood with my eyes closed, I wondered what in the world they could have in the garage for me. Then I was instructed to open my eyes, and there it was! The most thoughtful, sweetest gift anyone had ever given me!

Mark was into woodworking and had planned with the girls and made a beautiful, exquisitely constructed cedar chest! The looks on their faces told me how proud they were, and the three of them smiling at me told me how lucky I was. They showed it off to me: the cedar-lined inside complete with brass hinges, how the lid closed so snugly and the beautiful footings. The best part, they told me, was on the bottom. As the three carefully tilted the chest, I saw the wonderful inscription.

To me, from my hubby, a forever note that will always serve to remind the cedar chest's owner that it was a gift of love. No matter its contents or where it resides, my cedar chest will always carry with it the memories of that wonderful Christmas morning, when life slowed down a little, and the caring nature of family once again made a beautiful memory.

Déjà Vu Christmas

PAULA MUNIER

You can blame it on Hurricane Irene. At the University of Connecticut, my son Mikey lost power for a week at the house he rented with his college buddies. Back home at the little lakeside cottage in Massachusetts where I raised him, I had no lights or fans or water for five days of sweltering August heat. And out West in the air-conditioned cool of Phoenix, my ex-husband Michael worried and waited for his son to call him back and let him know he was okay.

That was his first mistake. Well, hardly his first mistake—more like his hundredth, thousandth, millionth mistake over the course of the twenty-five years in which I'd known him. But who's counting.

Teenage boys do not return phone calls. Given sufficient motivation, they may deign to return a parent's text via their smart phone, that motivation typically being the threatened loss of said smart phone.

But apparently Michael hadn't figured that out yet. So, in desperation, he broke the first of the many unspoken rules that had governed our relationship since we divorced nearly a dozen years before.

He called me.

This was highly irregular. All our communication was initially conducted through lawyers, and then, eventually, as passions and prejudices faded, through the occasional email. Phone calls were only permitted when Mikey was 35,000 feet in the air, hurtling toward one coast (mine) or the other (his), and the plane was late.

But Mikey was not en route at the moment.

I was sitting in my bed alone in absolute darkness, bored and hot and aching for a cold shower, when I saw the words *My Ex* appear on my cell as the first ring shattered the dark silence of the night. (Originally, the words that indicated my ex was calling were, shall we say, less neutral, but Mikey noticed and reprogrammed my phone. Like many children of divorce, he is, within the context of our broken nuclear family, the smart one.)

I was not pleased.

But after acknowledging that a natural disaster may indeed trump a delayed flight, I picked up, bracing for the sound of the only voice on the planet that could strike me dumb with fury.

"It's me," he said.

"Uh-huh," I said.

"Are you all right?"

"Fine." *Fine.* Every woman's favorite four-letter word.

"With the storm, I thought—"

"Fine," I repeated. "No power but fine."

"And Mikey? I haven't heard from Mikey."

"He doesn't have power either, but he's fine."

"What can I do?"

I bit back the wicked words that bounded into my throat and swallowed my bitterness. "Nothing. Really. We're fine."

My ex paused. "So I'm guessing everything's fine."

I laughed.

He always could make me laugh. It's not that he was really funny; *funny* was not the first word most people would use to describe an intense, taciturn guy like Michael. But whenever we were together, he had a tender way of teasing me that disarmed and charmed me every time. That playfulness, coupled with a passion that never failed to surprise and delight us both, made ours the one relationship we'd come to measure every other against. I'd had a husband before him and a couple of almost-husbands after him, but Michael remained the one significant other in my life who felt like home.

You can never go home again, which is why I'd moved to Massachusetts when we broke up. I took his son with me, and broke Michael's heart a second time. I did what I believed I had to do to save us from one another; in the end, all that playfulness and passion couldn't offset the mundane challenges that can undermine any couple—communication, money, teenagers. We both had kids from our first marriages, and they weren't exactly thrilled when we got married. And though they *were* thrilled when we had Mikey, even he couldn't save our not-so-blended family.

With enough time and distance, I thought I'd get over Michael. And I thought Michael would get over me—or die trying, as men are wont to do. But when he went off and got married to a Skinny-Mini-Me, I wasn't so sure.

Now he was single again—that marriage having died an inevitable death (she says with some satisfaction)—and I was single still. He was alone in his bed—and I was alone in mine. He was teasing me—and I was laughing.

You know what happened next. We talked all night and all day and all night again. He said he was sorry and I said I was sorry and he said he'd always loved me and I said I'd always loved him and he said we're older and wiser now and I said: *Are we really?*

By the time the lights were back on, so were we. More than a decade of rancor and regret forgotten as we reminded each other why we'd been so good together all those years ago. Flush with muscle memory, our hearts remembered what our brains had vowed to forget. Over the course of two months and a million phone calls, texts and emails, we were in love. Again.

It was like being struck by lightning a second time; already inured to the shock, we felt only a strong afterglow. And in the warmth of that afterglow, we made plans. Serious plans. We arranged to meet face-to-face somewhere in the middle of the country after Christmas for what would be only the third time in eleven years—a sort of trial run. In the meantime, Michael started looking for a new job on the East Coast.

In a mere matter of days, he garnered the interest of a big firm. They were flying him out for an interview. By now it was early November—and Christmas was just around the corner. Christmas, the time of year when I was the most sentimental, the most vulnerable, the most emotional. The time of year when I was most likely to do something very, very stupid.

We didn't tell anyone.

"I want to keep us to ourselves for a while," I told Michael, but in truth I was too scared to tell my friends or family, most of whom had held my hand through the divorce, the custody battle and the acrimonious aftermath. I wanted to live in this lovely bubble a little longer.

Then the past weighed in—and I panicked. Driving to work in my Jeep the day before Michael was due to arrive for his interview, I played our song, which I am embarrassed to admit is that lame Foreigner song "I Don't Want to Live Without You." (What can I say; it was the eighties.)

I was giddy at the thought of seeing him. Too giddy. Dangerously giddy.

I'd felt this way before—and it had taken me a lot of years and a lot of yoga to get over it. What was I thinking? I flipped off the iPod and burst into tears. Sobs, really. I wept so wildly that I couldn't see the road.

There was a Dunkin' Donuts on the corner. (There is a Dunkin' Donuts on virtually every corner in the great Commonwealth of Massachusetts; we invented it.) I pulled into the parking lot and sat there, engine idling, until I'd cried myself out. Then I texted Michael: Tell me this is real.

He texted me right back: It's real. C u tomorrow.

I took a deep breath, and then did what any self-respecting woman planning to win back her ex would do: I called in sick and went and got a mani-pedi.

The next day I was at the airport early. Twitchy, jittery, silly. It was unseemly in a woman my age. I was a grandmother, for God's sake.

I closed my eyes and thought of my granddaughters. I smiled to myself.

I opened my eyes, and there he was. Long and nearly as lean as he'd been when I'd married him twenty-five years before. Well, that was one of us. I smiled to myself again.

Michael loped over, his dark blue eyes never leaving mine. He grinned, took me in his arms and that was that. Once again, he was the man who'd called me his Marilyn Monroe—and I was the woman who'd called him my Heathcliff.

***

He got the job. The offer letter came December 9, the same day I got laid off. Serendipity? Karma? Blind luck? Whatever you called it, to us it seemed as if this was meant to be. I was home with nothing to do but worry, so I made the ultimate sacrifice and started clearing out closets to make room for Michael. A week later, he packed up his truck and started driving east.

It was time to start telling people. First, our son, Mikey, who was still away at school. I would've preferred to tell him in person, but by the time he came home for Christmas break his father would already be here. I tried calling, but of course he didn't answer. This was a text message waiting to happen.

Mom: Your father is coming home.

Son: y

Mom: We've reconciled.

Son: srsly?

Mom: Seriously. What do you think?

Son: idk

Mom: I know it's unexpected.

Son: meh

Mom: What?

Son: whatever

That wasn't so bad. Emboldened by Mikey's lackluster response, I called my mother in Las Vegas.

"Hi, Mom," I said.

"What's wrong?" My mother always knew when something was up.

"I've got good news and bad news," I said. "Or bad news and bad news, depending on how you look at it."

"What's wrong?" she repeated.

"I got laid off."

"Oh, honey, I am so sorry. What is wrong with those people?"

"I should have looked harder for another job." I paused. "I'm looking now."

"What's the good news?"

"I hope you'll see it as good news."

"What's wrong?"

"Michael and I have reconciled."

"Oh, for Christ's sake," she said.

I laughed. "He got a job here and is on his way right now."

I could hear the wheels turning in my mother's mind. "It's a good position?"

"It's a good position."

"Hmph." My mother paused. "So maybe he's your blessing in disguise."

***

News travels fast among siblings. I didn't have to tell my older children; Mikey told them for me. By the time we all got together at a diner for dinner, they were ready to discuss their mother's folly as if I weren't even there.

Mikey: It's the yoga. When Mom became a yoga teacher, she completely changed. All she talks about now is love and forgiveness and redemption. She really believes in all that stuff.

Mom: I'm right here, you know.

Greg: You're totally wrong, Mikey. I don't think Mom's changed at all. This proves it. She's just repeating her old patterns. She's stuck.

Mom: I can hear you.

Alexis: Mom's getting old and we're all gone and she's all alone and miserable. She just wants to be happy. Give her a break. What do you care what she does?

Mom: Thanks, honey. I think.

***

With the big reveal safely behind me, I took my old, deluded, stuck yoga self home to meditate upon my past patterns and future follies. Five days, 2,727 miles and two new tires later, my blessing in disguise rolled up to the garden fence that fronted our little cottage in his beloved F-150 truck.

He kissed me. I laughed.

It was our déjà vu Christmas all over again.

LOVE NEVER DIES

NORMA JEAN THORNTON

Returning from a meeting in the middle of December and listening to a poignant rendition of "White Christmas" on the radio, I took a detour to look at Christmas lights. Suddenly I found myself driving by the restaurant where my husband and I had had our first date over forty years ago. As I slowly drove home alone through the rain, memories of the past took over.

If this were only nine years ago, a fire would be roaring in the fireplace because he knew it made me happy, and I'd be walking into a nice, warm, toasty house. Tonight, I blink through tears, knowing I'll have to light the pinecones and wood for myself when I get home. *But do I really want a fire?* Watching the flames no longer warms me the way it did then, and it hurts my heart.

In the past, I'd pull into the driveway and see two pairs of tiny, shiny eyes staring out at me from the small arched windows, just as they do tonight: two of our cats sit in the windowsills in the den and peek through curtains, waiting for me to come inside. He said they seemed to know exactly when I was due home from work, because every day at the same time, that's where they'd be.

The cats are still looking out the window, waiting for me each time I come home, but there's no fire to greet me, to warm my heart and soul, and no husband with a welcome-home bear hug.

I go inside, and the memories continue flooding back as I feed the cats. My thoughts wander back to that last Christmas season, and our final three days together, especially our last night.

***

Even though he was as excited about each present as the kids were and enjoyed Christmas, every year he would lightly grumble and grouse and complain about everything, including the stockings that were filled with goodies. He'd always mumble *"The Grinch had it right!"*

This was a second marriage for both of us, bringing a total of six kids to the family, so at Christmas eight stockings were always hung. However, one Christmas, one stocking was missing. Although I had filled his, I didn't hang it that year, waiting for his response. When he couldn't find it, he asked hesitantly, "Where's my stocking?"

I commented: "I thought you didn't want one."

Early in our relationship, he had found that rather than actually apologizing for anything minor, all he had to do was give me that apologetic look and pout, the way a little kid would, and it worked every time . . . melted my heart and always got a smile from me.

This time, like a shy little boy with his lower lip in that deliberately exaggerated, yet endearing pout and those pleading green eyes in the way that always tugged at my heartstrings, he sheepishly responded: "You know I don't really mean that."

He was right; he didn't mean it. But each year after that, we played the game, and he had to hunt for his stocking, as though it were an Easter egg, and he loved it.

But his last year, it was different…In the beginning of December, he was brought home by ambulance from his latest, and final, stay in the hospital. Complications of the cancer that was ravaging his gorgeous body had kept him there for six weeks this time.

As the attendants wheeled him through the house to his newly set-up hospice bed, he kept repeating, "I really didn't mean to be the Grinch and spoil Christmas. I really didn't. I'm so sorry."

He wasn't a Grinch and never could be, but he loved the Grinch, and had called himself that every year—another little game we played. The kids had even bought him a stuffed Grinch one year.

We all knew he didn't mean it, but now it bothered him more and more each day, especially since I hadn't done a thing yet for Christmas. Every other year by this time the house would smell good from homemade candy and cinnamon-spiced pinecones and be over-decorated with poinsettias, garlands and wreaths, with stuffed teddy bears, snowmen, Santas and elves sitting everywhere.

He would already—grudgingly, yet willingly—have put up the tree and added the lights, while I was busy making hot chocolate, playing Christmas music and pestering him to sing along with me, to keep him motivated, until it was my turn with the tree, to decorate it. His only job was to put the tree up and gladly take it down.

Suddenly, on the morning of December 10, he blurted out, "I don't want Christmas to be any different than before. Promise me you won't change anything; do everything just like you've always done."

Completely confined to the bed, he feverishly focused on how Christmas should be, and hurriedly continued to tell me what he wanted done. Christmas 2005 would be his doing, even though he knew his time was quickly fading, and he wouldn't be there by Christmas Day.

"Be sure to have turkey, with your cornbread and wild rice dressing, mashed potatoes and gravy, and your sweet potatoes. And this time, don't forget the cranberry sauce!

"All the salsa, dips and chips, and everything else you always fix. Don't leave out anything...be sure to have beans and your bean dip. Everybody loves that.

"I want the tree decorated in red, white and green; same with the wrapping paper. Use paper plates and plastic forks . . . and this time, throw them away after dinner; don't wash 'em and save 'em like you always do.

"And make lots of candy, with nuts . . . especially the peanut butter fudge."

***

His hospice bed had been set up in the den, his favorite room, close to his TV. It was also near where we always put the Christmas tree, so I shoved my way through stuff that had been piled in the shed, to find the fake tree. While two of our boys worked on putting it up, I made a quick trip to Walmart for paper products and decorations.

Not wanting to be away from him one second longer than I had to, I rushed through the store, throwing everything red, white and green that I could find into the cart.

When I got back to the house, I dropped everything at the foot of his bed. I sat next to him and pulled each item from the bags. He tried to show interest, but he was so ill he couldn't even raise his head from the pillow and listlessly nodded his approval. He halfheartedly watched as four of the older granddaughters decorated the tree with red and white lights, red and white garlands, and red, white and green glittery ornaments.

I hastily dug through the myriad of Christmas stuff from years past to find his favorite ornament and added it to the tree: we had bought it in Hawaii in 1996. It was Santa and Mrs. Claus kissing on a surfboard. Santa was dressed in a red and white surfing outfit; Mrs. Claus in a white muumuu with red and green poinsettias and a red poinsettia lei around her head. He always said it reminded him of us.

The daughters set out the red poinsettia table centerpiece and white sparkly place mats with a red-and-green poinsettia design and red cloth napkins. Matching salt-and-pepper shakers and coasters were added to the table, along with fat red candles.

Everything would be as normal as possible for him, under the circumstances, with me on autopilot. I pulled the Christmas stockings out and hung his at the foot of his bed, and a granddaughter found his stuffed Grinch. When we put it next to him, he accepted it with a tentative, little lopsided grin.

***

He was adamant about having a clock and a light beside him at all times those last three days. His last night, just as the sun went down, and every thirty minutes or so afterwards, he asked, "What time is it?" He asked the time more frequently as the night went on. At 10:15 p.m., December 11, he frantically said, "It's time—quick, everyone come here . . . Hurry, hurry . . . Come on, little girls. Hurry!"

My sister, all six of our kids and four of the fourteen grandkids were there. He told each of them how much he loved them, how important each of them was to him and how proud of them he was. He kissed them all, and there wasn't a dry eye on any of us.

After his turn with the kids, he turned to me and said, "Come closer!"

I scooted as close as possible to him, but he kept saying "Closer!"

Crying silently, I crawled into bed with him, trying to get as close as I could. But he angrily said, "You're not the real Normie . . . Where's my Normie? . . . I want my Normie." His vision was all but gone by that time, and his eyes were clouded over. As his pain meds were rapidly increased, he was going in and out of consciousness, and it was impossible to tell whether it was him or the meds talking.

I kept repeating, "It's me, Honey." I finally straddled him on the bed, and I leaned down, holding his face in my hands, and kissed him. "What do I need to do to prove I'm me?"

I had on a lightweight button-up pajama top, and he put his hands to my chest, his fingers fumbling as he unbuttoned the thing, and said, "Ahh . . . that's my Normie." He took me in his hands and nuzzled his face into me.

He had rarely called me Normie in the past—maybe two or three times. I have no idea why he did then.

Everyone had already gone into the living room, allowing us to be alone, although they were still close enough to see and hear what was happening. I whispered, "Honey—all the kids are in the other room and can see what you're doing!"

He loudly said, "That's their problem!" as he moved his hands all over me and nuzzled me more.

Sometimes there's nothing one can do but laugh, even at the most horrible of times. That time brought a nervous laugh from everyone.

He kept repeating, "I love you, I love you. I'm so sorry I'm leaving you. I'm not going to be here to protect you."

Heartbroken, and knowing it was little consolation, I tried to reassure him: "Don't worry about that . . . Just remember, I love you with all my heart and always will."

He stayed with us for another five hours, going in and out of consciousness. He didn't ask for the time again, but at midnight, three hours before he died, he suddenly said, "Would you marry me again?"

Of course, I said, "Yes!" not realizing he meant right then, at that moment. I thought he was asking if I would do it all over again.

To my surprise, he hurriedly told me, "Give me a ring, quick, give me a ring!"

I took the wedding ring that had been my mother's from my left index finger, expecting him to put it back on that finger, but when I offered it, he said, "Give me the right finger—your ring one!"

During his last conversations with everyone that night, his voice was high-pitched and rushed, his sentences short, choppy and erratic. It was obvious that medication played a big part, but he was fighting to stay in control, even through the haze of mind-muddling drugs and the cancer. Because his actions had been so unpredictable, and we thought that his vision was completely gone, I was amazed that he had realized that it wasn't my ring finger. As he lay in bed, I held out the correct finger for him, without taking my original wedding set off. Without a word, and with his hands shaking, he took my hand and placed the ring on my finger.

I kissed him and said, "I love you." He closed his eyes and, less than three hours later, he was gone. My husband proposed twice, thirty years apart, and put a ring on my finger each time. There may not have been a second wedding ceremony, but it double-sealed the bonds from the first. Both rings will stay on that finger forever.

ABOUT THE
CONTRIBUTORS

DAWN ARMSTRONG

A charitable blog correspondent, Dawn wanders the world in search of time travel, danger, eternal love, all of which contribute to the scenes and content of her inspirational books and novels. Dawn's first book, *Sensations: A Little Book of Love . . .*, spreads hope around the globe. Don't miss her exciting new paranormal romance, *Knower*. To learn more, visit her at www.littlebookoflove.net and www.theknower.wordpress.com.

JENNIFER BERN BASYE

A *New York Times* bestselling author and former Random House senior editor, Jennifer is the mother of two amazing sons. She teaches publishing skills and nonfiction writing, coaches writers, and runs writing retreats in Lake Tahoe and on her great-grandfather's farm in Washington state. Learn more about her retreats at www.writebythelake.com or www.writeatthefarm.com.

SHERYL J. BIZE BOUTTE

Sheryl is a Northern California writer and management consultant. More of her short stories, poetry and commentary can be seen at www.sjbb-talkinginclass.blogspot.com/.

RUTH BREMER

Ruth is a freelance writer, blogger and aspiring novelist. Her stupefying brilliance can be found at www.insightfulish.com.

ABOUT THE CONTRIBUTORS

KATHRYN CANAN

Whenever the family cabin in Montana is buried in snow, Kathryn Canan and her husband live in California with two psychotic cats. She is a freelance writer, Latin tutor, and early music teacher and performer. She has recorded CDs of medieval and Renaissance music with Briddes Roune and the New Queen's Ha'penny Consort. Her master's thesis on Anglo-Saxon medicine has made her one of the few experts in diseases caused by malevolent elves.

CHERIE CARLSON

Cherie Carlson has lived in Northern California for 37 years. The joys of her life are her four children and nine grandchildren, to whom she is "Ranna." A full-time caregiver to her husband, she is also a part-time Realtor. In her spare time she is working on a homeschooling blog and a parent curriculum for homeschoolers.

MELISSA CHAMBERS

Melissa Chambers comes from a family of writers. She has taught elementary school for more than 25 years and loves teaching Writing Workshop to her wonderful third grade class. An animal lover since she was given a Banty chick at age two, she has been involved in animal rescue for 10 years. Currently working on a novel, she is also collaborating with her husband on a book of short stories about the many special-needs Chihuahuas they have known and loved.

SCOTT "ROBBY" EVANS

Scott (aka Robby) Evans is happily married and has three sons. He teaches writing at the University of the Pacific in Stockton, CA. His new, somewhat romantic psychological thriller, *Sylvia's Secret,* was published by Port Yonder Press in 2013. It is the third in a series of "literary" murder mysteries.

NEVA J. HODGES

Neva belongs to California Writers Club Tri-Valley Branch and was membership chair for three years. She has been published in the Oakland Senior Anthology and the local newspaper for a real-life story. Currently she is writing short stories and a novel.

JULAINA KLEIST-CORWIN

Julaina is a creative writing instructor for the City of Dublin, California. She has won first place awards in short story contests and published in several anthologies by the S.F. Writers Conference and Las Positas College, and is a field supervisor for intern teachers. You can find her blogging at timetowritenow.blogspot.com or her website at julaina.homestead.com.

CHELS KNORR

Chels Knorr is an editor, writer and student. Her favorite things include traveling, walks with her dog, Goose, a competitive game of Scrabble and chocolate chip waffles. Sometimes she posts ramblings at chelsknorr.com.

DENA KOUREMETIS

Consumer journalist, author and would-be shrink Dena Kouremetis loves to examine life from a midlife perspective. She is a professional blogger for *Forbes Magazine* and a national Lady Boomer examiner for Examiner.com. She has authored, co-authored and contributed content to dozens of books, and loves to speak to groups about how our online presence says volumes about us. She welcomes visits to her website at www.communic8or.com.

CHARLES KUHN

Charles Kuhn is an accomplished writer in the areas of mystery, nonfiction and adventure. He has published short stories in various magazines, self-published and writes for local writers groups, including the poetry group for the local Sacramento Multiple Sclerosis Association. Mr. Kuhn and his wife reside in Citrus Heights, CA.

APRIL KUTGER

April Kutger, an award-winning author of fiction and nonfiction who, when she's not writing, volunteers as a basic skills tutor and swims on a Masters team. Christmas Eve with her three children and ten grandchildren is her favorite day of the year.

LELIA KUTGER

Lelia Torluemke Kutger Fettes was born in 1917 in St. Louis, MO, the granddaughter of German immigrants. She met Joseph Kutger when she was working as a telephone operator in Fort Dix, NJ. They married in 1942. While going through an old box of papers many decades later, she found the telegram she received telling her that her husband was missing in action. It inspired her to collaborate with her daughter about what she went through during the war.

SUZANNE LILLY

Suzanne writes lighthearted stories with a splash of suspense, a flash of the unexplained, a dash of romance and always a happy ending. Her debut novel was *Shades of the Future* in 2012 followed by *Untellable* in 2013. Her short stories have appeared in numerous places online and in print. She lives in Northern California where she reads, writes, cooks, swims and teaches elementary students. To find out more visit her author page at http://www.suzannelilly.com, her blog at http://www.teacherwriter.net, her Facebook page at www.facebook.com/SuzanneLillyAuthor and follow her on Twitter @SuzanneLilly.

PAULA MUNIER

Paula Munier is a writer, teacher and content strategist who's authored or co-authored a number of books, including the acclaimed memoir *Fixing Freddie: A True Story about a Boy, a Mom, and the Very, Very Bad Beagle Who Saved Them* and *5-Minute Mindfulness: Simple Daily Shortcuts to Transform Your Life*. She lives in New England with her ex-husband, a relationship best described by her Facebook status: It's Complicated.

MARSHA PORTER

Marsha Porter mastered the art of the 500-word essay when such compositions were the punishment du jour at her parochial grade school. She has since published over 200 articles and an annual movie review guide. Her short stories have won numerous awards.

CHRISTINA RICHTER

Christina and her husband Mark have been married 26 years and live in Northern California. Her two daughters are off to college but they still love to surprise her with special Christmas presents. Christina is a writer; her current project is the history of the Roseville Fiddyment family, a gold rush era story that continues to this day.

MARGARET H. SCANLON

Margaret is a longtime resident of Hamburg, New York.

JACK SKILLICORN

Jack Skillicorn was born in 1933 in Watsonville, California where he grew up, worked and attended Monterey Peninsula College. He studied, played football, dropped out and joined the USAF during the Korean conflict for 4 years, then out 4 years, then returned to the USAF during the Vietnam conflict, and then back to college for a BS in Accounting. Jack was first published in the *California County* journal of the County Supervisor's Association of California with an article called, "Who said you could run a county like a Business?" In retirement he began writing family stories for grandchildren and family.

JUDY STEVENS

Judy Stevens enjoys blowing the dumb blonde stereotype out of the water with a masters degree in education, and as the mom of five, Judy voices her opinion whenever possible. Writing is a passion. She started writing with an eye to the future and authoring a parenting book.

ILLIA THOMPSON

Illia Thompson, a graduate of Antioch College in Ohio, teaches memoir writing throughout the Monterery Peninsula and presents private journaling workshops. She received Honorable Mention in Writer's Digest Poetry Contests and has been published in poetry magazines. Her books include *Gracious Seasons,* about her journey through the last year of her husband's cancer, as well as *Heartframes,* collected poetry. Her most recent book, *Along the Memoir Way,* holds poems followed by blank pages, a workbook for memories. She resides in Carmel Valley, California.

NORMA JEAN THORNTON

Her baby sister called her Nonie, her great granddaughter calls her GumGum. Norma Jean Thornton, aka Noniedoodles and Granny-GumGum, is a rhyming, art-doodling, writing granny from Rio Linda, California, with four cats. She has self-published two books through lulu.com: *Nonie's 1st Big Bottom Girls' Rio Linda CookBook* and *Doodles & Rhymes: Noniedoodles, Volumes 1, 2 & 3.* As Granny-GumGum, Norma also writes children's truth-based animal stories, a variety of fun rhymes, and as The-Granny, is working with her cat, The-Windy, on *Nosie Rosie's Diary: The True "Tails" of a Very Special Kitty.* Norma Jean writes mainly nonfiction-Heinz-57-stuff, dabbling in everyday humor and more rhymes . . . then there's this rare, serious, emotional true story, "Love Never Dies." You can reach her at nooniedoodles@yahoo.com.

ABOUT THE CONTRIBUTORS

PAM WALTERS

Pam Walters spent 25 years as an ad agency copywriter. Since then, she's self-published *Become The Person You Were Created To Be* and *The Out Of Work Coloring Book.* Pam lives in Carmel, CA.

JERRY WHITE

After a career in the military and in real estate, Jerry now teaches in the Earth Science department of a community college.

TERI WILSON

Teri Wilson grew up as an only child and could often be found with her head in a book, lost in a world of romance and exotic places. As an adult, her love of books has led her to her dream career—writing for Harlequin Love Inspired and HQN. When Teri isn't traveling or writing, she enjoys knitting, painting and dancing, although she still hasn't quite mastered the tango. Teri lives in San Antonio, Texas, with her family and four sweet dogs, and loves to hear from readers! Visit her at www.teriwilson.net and be sure to look for her next book, *Unleashing Mr. Darcy,* coming from Harlequin HQN in January 2014.